"Strike Three!"

Photo by Steve Feldman

"Strike Three!"

A Player's Journey through the Infamous Baseball Strike of 1994

As told to
RUSS COHEN

Featuring
NIKCO RIESGO

Lulu.com
ISBN: 978-0-557-24643-4
© 2009 by Russ Cohen and Nikco Riesgo
Printed in the United States of America

To all of the players who sacrificed their careers during one of baseball's greatest time of need.

Contents

Acknowledgments ix

Foreword xi

Introduction: Russ Cohen xv

Introduction: Nikco Riesgo xvii

Nikco Timeline xx

Chapter 1: *Crossing the Picket Line* 1

Chapter 2: *The Business of Baseball* 9

Chapter 3: *Looking Back to 1994 and the Cancellation of the World Series* 15

Chapter 4: *When The Business Runs the Game* 23

Chapter 5: *The Call Up to the Expos* 29

Chapter 6: *The Final Days of the Montreal Expos* 35

Chapter 7: *Former Teammates Whose Paths Would Never Cross Again* 39

Chapter 8: *What's Next?* 43

Chapter 9: *Nikco's Connection with the Fans* 47

Chapter 10: *Mixed Messages* 51

Chapter 11: *Change Could Help the Game* 55

Chapter 12: *New Beginnings* 63

References 67

Index 69

Acknowledgments

I want to thank my wife Amy who is my constant source of inspiration. Thanks to my adopted dogs and cats for bringing joy into my life. Thanks to all of my friends and family who have supported me every step of the way. A special thanks to Laurie Hawkins, Michelle Riesgo, Matt Hirsch, Walik Edwards and Sumner Hunnewell, for their continued support.

Foreword

It's not very often that I do, but when a jackpot in a lottery grows large enough to pique my interest I always play the number 7440. An easy enough number to remember and even harder number for me to forget. It is a number that comes back to haunt me every April and remind me that I am no longer a fan of something I loved as a teenager.

Those four digits, in that exact order, starts a process in my head of dreaming of what could have been and what was ripped away and left for dead. It reminds me of untapped promise and stone cold greed. It brings back memories of baseball arguments with my father and friendship with pen pals and video tape traders from all over North America. Feelings of joy and pain all wrapped up with four awful numbers.

On August 12, 1994, Major League Baseball shut down its season and the premature close resulted in the cancellation of the remainder of the regular season as well as the playoffs and World Series. The strike/lockout/work stoppage, the fourth in 23 years, lasted 232 days and the cancellation of the 1994 Fall Classic was the first cancellation of a World Series since 1904. Owners cried poor and demanded a salary cap, while the Major League Baseball Players Association saw no reason to end a financial windfall that had seen salaries climb to dizzying heights. Discussion of Most Valuable Players and playoff match-ups were replaced with details of revenue-sharing, collusion, and federal mediators. The work stoppage was the final nail in the coffin for many baseball fans, many of whom vowed to never purchase another ticket.

The Montreal Expos, the baseball club I had rooted for and supported, sat atop the National League East with a record of 74-40 when the season was halted. The Expos were six games ahead of the Atlanta Braves and even more satisfying to this Philadelphia area resident, 20.5 games ahead of the Phillies. Montreal claimed the best record in Major League Baseball and was in the middle of their best season ever. Five Expos were named to the National League All-Star team. Young players were becoming stars and baseball media began to take notice making them favorites to represent the National League in the World Series. As history shows us, that never happened.

The Expos teams of the early 1980's were the teams that ignited my love for baseball. Tim Raines, my favorite ballplayer of all time, Gary Carter, Andre Dawson, Chris Speier, and Warren Cromartie were the players I followed from afar. In the days before the Internet, cell phones, and MLB Network, the only way a tween in southern New Jersey was going to truly follow the Expos was through video tape trading. I would dub Japanese cartoons and pro-wrestling video tapes and ship them to all parts of North America. In return, I would have my trading partners tape and send VHS recordings of Montreal Expos games. Sometimes these games were weeks, if not months behind, but it was the only way I could truly get my Expos fix. The underground taping communities helped to give me my first taste Jean-Pierre Roy and Dave Van Horne calling Expos games.

While those teams of the '80's will always have a place in my heart, they were always a step behind the Phillies. They seemed to consistently be missing that piece of the puzzle to take them to the next level. You knew they were good teams but they were never great and they never gave the feeling of "this is our year". The 1994 team? That was a different story.

When you look at the roster for the 1994 Expos, it was filled with ripe, young talent with a healthy splash of veteran know-how. The Expos farm system, considered one of the best in baseball, stocked the team with homegrown talent. The outfield of Larry Walker, Moises Alou, and Marquis Grissom was arguably the best in the game. The Expos bullpen was solid with John Wetteland and Mel Rojas and the starting rotation was in great shape with Jeff Fassero, Ken Hill and a rookie by the name of Pedro Martinez.

It felt like a winning team and it seemed like all the pieces had fallen into place. The best record in league, a six game lead over the Braves, and a team that was hitting their stride with September headed around the corner. For one fleeting moment in the summer of 1994, Expos fans could stick their chests out a little.

The work stoppage destroyed the Expos. When baseball returned, Larry Walker left for Colorado, John Wetteland was traded to the Yankees, Marquis Grissom was traded to Atlanta,

Moises Alou went south to Florida, and Pedro Martinez went on to Boston. By 1997, the Montreal Expos had gone on a door busting fire sale gutting the team of talent they could no longer afford. As the team's downward spiral on the field mounted, the chances for a new stadium slid along with the teams' performance. The team, my team, had gone from a World Series contender to a laughing stock in just under five years.

In almost every case, when a team loses in a championship series they lost to a better team. Yes, there are times when a team gets "hot" at the right time and manages to "steal" a championship but for the most part the better team wins. What if you never found out which team is better? What if the odds were finally stacked in your team's favor but you never played the championship games? What if your team didn't lose, but there were no winners? What if it was your turn to win and they decided not to play the game?

For me, baseball died on August 12, 1994. While the body of the Expos clung to life for a handful of years, the quality of life never returned. When the plug was finally pulled on October 3, 2004, the Expos last game before relocating to Washington D.C.; it was like I was saying a final goodbye to a friend with a long-term terminal illness. It was time to end the pain for both of us. My team was no more but those questions always remained in my head. What if there was labor peace in 1994? Would the Expos been able to hold off the Braves? What would it been like if they played baseball in Montreal... in October?

74-40. What could have been and what we will never know. Oh, how those numbers haunt me.

— **Michael McDonald,
Fox Sports Radio**

Russ Cohen (l), David Mantle (r)
at Topps Headquarters in New York City

Introduction: Russ Cohen

Growing up on Long Island gave me the joy of living in suburbia and yet I was close enough to the "Big City" so I could attend baseball games with my grandparents and my parents. The Mets were our team of choice and when I was a young pitcher I had dreams of being the next Tom Seaver. After beaning my best friend in Little League I lost the ability to throw strikes, and that's when I realized that this game was fun to play but it was a bit dangerous and that made me respect it tremendously.

Baseball was like a religion in my household and my mother would say that I would talk baseball 24-7 even at a very young age. At this point in my life I can write about one of the greatest sports on earth and it's something for which I have a passion. With the help of Doug Cataldo and later Dean Warr I started www.sportsology.net in 2000 and that's when I started to live out my dream. I always wanted to cover the sport in some way, shape or form, and now I get to do this on an every day basis. That has given me a lot of joy and it makes all those hours that I either sat in front of a television set or had a transistor radio up to my ear all worth it.

In this book I hope to give you some of my own personal experiences mixed in with some great insights from Nikco Riesgo and some biting quotes from fans, players and industry professionals.

This book covers everything baseball: the business, the players, relationships, the joy of winning and the sorrow of losing. As a youngster I was unable to walk and my parents knew there was a great chance that I would be wheelchair bound for my entire life. But they had other plans for me, and because of their perseverance and stick-to-itiveness, they found the right doctors who performed a landmark surgery on me that gave me the ability to walk just before kindergarten. I was unable to play in gym class with the other kids until third grade because the school was afraid my parents would sue if I got hurt. However, I was playing baseball after school hours thanks to my local Little League chapter. I will never forget those days and the joy it gave me when I played. I experienced that same joy in writing this book, and I hope you will get that same feeling after you finish it.

Nikco Riesgo, 1991, Montreal Expos

Introduction: Nikco Riesgo

I began playing baseball at the age of six. I didn't know all of the rules, but that didn't matter much. I just loved being dressed up in my uniform and wanted to hit the baseball every time I got up to bat. In those days we didn't have a coach pitch, so we had to hit our live pitching. It wasn't a very good experience since most pitchers couldn't throw strikes. Six inning games took nearly three hours to play. Everybody walked or got on by error. The good thing is that we got a chance to play and learn more about the "Game". I would have loved to pitch. That is the greatest position to play, if you get a chance. I realize now that I never got a chance because that is where all the coaches want their sons to play. So I began my baseball career at second base. This was fun. I loved to cover second when a runner would try to steal the base. From an early age, stealing bases and catching others trying to steal became one of the biggest thrills for me outside of hitting a home run.

Every chance we got we played pick-up games in the streets. Wiffle Ball for us meant we only needed a ball, a bat and two players. We would pitch to each other for a full nine innings of ball. There was no running so we didn't need bases. It was either a home run, double, or an out, depending on whether we hit the ball over the fence or off of it. Anything less was an out. We would play from 9 a.m. to 9 p.m. nonstop during the summer months. We never got tired. We played a whole seven game World Series event. We actually became the real MLB players in our imagination. This visualization of success at an early age became a part of my mentality and would later become a part of my reality.

Baseball became a fantasy world for me to escape to. Whenever I played the game, I became the greatest player in the history of the world. It was so awesome because I had a billion fans all over the world on TV cheering for me, real MLB Star names, and play-by-play Howard Cosell impersonations. This was far superior to Playstation and XBox of today's generation. This was playing the "Game" live at its ultimate levels. When I wrote my first book at age 7, my teacher asked me within the 'about the author' section, "What do I want to do when I grow up? I wrote that I would play Major League Baseball.

The "Game" absolutely consumed me. Every stat, every homer, every strikeout became memorized. I noticed that memorizing and calculating my baseball numbers improved my real math in school. Math became a whiz for me. All my other studies became simple for me as well because I began learning to concentrate at the highest precise levels of concentration.

When I came up to bat, I just knew I would get a hit somewhere. There was no way I would strike out. That was my mentality. I believed I would never strike out against anybody. So I dug in real good at the plate to hit the ball hard and let it rip. My goal was to score two runs every game – by any means possible. With every walk or hit, I was determined to steal second and third and even home if I could. I made it my responsibility to score two runs myself, and drive in as many runs as possible with me.

By the time I reached High School, I was ready for the chance to be one of the greatest. I followed the footsteps of the young Hall of Famer, Tony Gwynn, at the renowned Long Beach Poly High. His father, Charles Gwynn, Sr. was a coach for me growing up and I will never forget him. At practice, we would work so hard and run all day. We never lost a single game that I played for him.

I earned the National High School Scholar Athlete Award playing both football and baseball while graduating with a 3.98 GPA.

I became an All-American at San Diego St. University and hit over .400 as a sophomore.

I signed to play the "Game" as a pro after my junior year in quest of my ultimate goal - The World Series Ring!

Nikco Timeline

April 1985: Named National High School Scholar Athlete with a 3.98 GPA.

June 3, 1985: Drafted by the Milwaukee Brewers in the 25th round of the 1985 amateur draft, but did not sign.

August 1986: Named Freshman All-American at San Diego St. University.

August 1987: Hits over .400 as sophomore at San Diego St. University.

June 1, 1988: Drafted by the San Diego Padres in the 8th round of the 1988 amateur draft.

September 1988: Leads Spokane Indians to Northwest League Championship.

January 5, 1990: Traded by the San Diego Padres to the New York Mets for Craig Repoz (minors).

September 1990: Voted MVP of the Florida State League as a member of the St. Lucie Mets.

August 30, 1990: Traded by the New York Mets with Rocky Elli (minors) to the Philadelphia Phillies for Tom Herr.

December 3, 1990: Drafted by the Montreal Expos from the Philadelphia Phillies in the 1990 Rule V draft.

April 21, 1991: Makes MLB debut with the Montreal Expos vs. St. Louis Cardinals.

May 8, 1991: Returned (earlier draft pick) by the Montreal Expos to the Philadelphia Phillies.

May 9, 1991: Hits 14 home runs for the AA Reading Phillies.

April 1, 1992: Released from the Philadelphia Phillies and signs with the Kansas City Royals as minor league free agent.

August, 1992: Sold from the Kansas City Royals to the Saltillo (Mexican) in an unknown transaction. *(Date given is approximate. Exact date is uncertain.)*

May 14, 1993: Signed as a Free Agent with the Milwaukee Brewers. Leads El Paso Diablos to Texas League Championship Series.

December 14, 1993: Sent by the Milwaukee Brewers to the Detroit Tigers to complete an earlier deal made on August 28, 1993. The Milwaukee Brewers sent a player to be named later to the Detroit Tigers for Ron Rightnowar. The Milwaukee Brewers sent Nikco Riesgo (December 14, 1993) to the Detroit Tigers to complete the trade.

August 15, 1994: Major League Baseball Players go on strike.

September 14, 1994: The World Series is cancelled for the first time since 1904.

March 1995: Reports to training camp with the Montreal Expos as a replacement player.

March 1995: Traded to the Boston Red Sox during spring training.

March 20, 1995: The owner of the Baltimore Orioles, Peter Angelos, cancels the remainder of his team's spring training games.

April, 1 1995: The Red Sox give him his unconditional release.

May 1995: Played for the Alexandria Aces of the Texas-Louisiana League (independent).

June 1995: Played for the Laredo Apaches of the Texas-Louisiana League (independent).

July 1995: Played for the Lubbock Crickets of the Texas-Louisiana League (independent). Wins Texas-Louisiana League Championship.

October 1995: Nikco Riesgo hangs up his spikes for the last time.

September 29, 2004: The Montreal Expos played their last-ever game.

January 11, 2008: Nikco launches www.mlpo.org to promote youth baseball.

Chapter 1

Crossing the Picket Line

"I had been reading in the newspapers and following the stories that this had been one of the suggestions as a possibility," Riesgo said, talking about possible replacement players. "I didn't know for sure and I had no idea that they would go in that direction. But I knew for sure when they gave me the call."

Damon Nikco Riesgo is a prideful man. He worked hard to get where he was in the sport of baseball, but never got his big break to be an everyday player in Major League Baseball.

In 1994, the owners of Major League Baseball wanted to change the economic landscape of their business relationship with the players, with a salary cap being the centerpiece for their new business plan. The ball was firmly in the court of the players to either accept the salary cap or call for a strike, and they spent a great deal of time holed up in a Chicago hotel holding the fate of future players and the current season in their hands.

In situations where the business side of sports took precedence over the game itself, fans and the media generally tended to choose a side, sticking firmly with that decision for the duration of the disagreement.

In the court of public opinion, the fans didn't want a strike. They didn't care about salary caps or anything other than wanting to see the players play. However, they couldn't help but wonder. Why the 1994 season was in jeopardy so late in the campaign?

Where the business of the game was concerned, the owners clearly made good money from regular season tickets, and for those teams who made the playoffs, they can charge two or three times the regular season ticket price. It's a sports rite of passage for fans to pack their stadiums and arenas during the post-season. Baseball fans are more than happy to pay the exorbitant prices because their team has a chance to win the World Series while giving them bragging rights which carries over into the following season. They also get to buy some great championship swag, with the proceeds from these sales going squarely into the owner's pockets. The players knew that the owners had more to lose in 1994 and they were prepared to play that card while damning any consequences.

"I was over covering the All-Star game in 1994 for WDEL radio, and we were at the hotel in Pittsburgh, and the players were talking about going on strike sometime in August because they were unhappy with the collective bargaining agreement, and we were standing outside of the conference room," longtime Phillies beat writer Jeff Winokur began, "Ozzie Smith had come outside. Tom Glavine came outside, and Glavine went to the microphones and said, 'You know what this is what we are doing. If we don't get a deal by.....' I think it was August 14, they were going to strike on August 15."

Even the working media were in disbelief that a strike could actually happen and the biggest post-season in sports at that time, being that the World Series had the popularity edge over the NFL's Super Bowl, had a chance to be canceled because of greed.

Neither side was hurting for money, but the owners wanted a salary cap they never got. Several years later, they settled on a "luxury tax", which penalizes teams that spend beyond a fixed limit and funnels that extra cash down to the "small market" clubs. Only a handful of teams pay into this tax every season, and the system (with its many pros and cons making it imperfect at best), there still seemed to be no sensible point to stopping the season, even if this was what they came up with as an alternative solution.

"Everyone didn't believe baseball would strike that late in the year where they would possibly lose the World Series, and we asked Glavine basically: what is precipitating this now? Why not wait until Spring Training?" said Winokur, who summarized, "They thought because of the World Series, this may be a way to force the owners' hand and make them come up with a deal so they wouldn't lose a World Series, and as we know they lost the World Series that year.

"I made sure that on August the 12th we went to Yankee Stadium (they were playing the Red Sox), bought a ticket and we (he and his son Andrew) went to the game, and I told everybody this is going to be the last baseball game that I ever pay for, and it sure enough was and we saw Yankees-Red Sox, and the next day they went on strike."

When the league's fourth in-season labor stoppage started August 12, 1994 (MLB's eighth stoppage overall) fans, owners, and players were still hopeful there would be a post-season and a World Series. However, when everything was definitively cancelled for the first time in the history of the sport due to a work stoppage, the owners sprung into action, declaring that there would be players to open Spring Training in 1995. They would be known as "replacement players".

"I had been reading in the newspapers and following the stories that this had been one of the suggestions as a possibility," Riesgo said, talking about the plan for replacement players. "I didn't know for sure and I had no idea that they would go in that direction.

"But I knew for sure when they gave me the call. I was really hoping they would give me a call because it would give me an opportunity to communicate my concerns about how this would impact my union status. I didn't decide to cross until I knew for sure the union wasn't going to do anything to protect me."

This slugging outfielder had a hard choice to make but, when push came to shove, he had a chance and he took it. There was a concern that there might be angry fans holding signs ridiculing players crossing the picket lines or, even more daunting, striking Major League players expressing their displeasure up close and personal.

"It was the Expos that I went into camp with. I believe I was the first to cross and I believe later on that some lefty crossed," he stated and added that he was very surprised that there weren't any players or fans picketing. "No, it wasn't like that. We were kind of anticipating that kind of an ugly scene. The picket lines and the major league players out there. Fans out there throwing tomatoes at me, doing things like that. It really wasn't like that.

"The Expos invited all minor-leaguers to camp like it was a normal Spring Training. So it really had the appearance of a normal Spring Training. It wasn't really announced who was going to play during the games, so that was kept under wraps. Of course nobody knew who was going to cross the line and who was there for minor leagues. It was very, very inconspicuous."

It was anything but a normal Spring Training.

The Detroit Tigers gave manager Sparky Anderson a pass, he didn't want to coach "replacement players" and he didn't have to and his job was still safe since he had led the Tigers to a title in 1984.

"He was one of the smartest guys I've seen in baseball," said Riesgo, who ran into Anderson when he was a AA player in the Tigers organization along with sluggers Bobby Higginson and Tony Clark, each who had over 700 RBI in the big leagues.

Toronto Blue Jays' manager Cito Gaston worked it out so he didn't have to work with these players. They all had fancy assignment names, but the feeling out there was that many of these players, including Dennis "Oil Can" Boyd, knew they were taking a big chance, and they might not be able to get a job once the strike was over because of these feelings.

On March 20, Baltimore Orioles owner Peter Angelos cancelled the remainder of Spring Training games for a variety of reasons. The main reason being, he didn't want to use replacement players. Even local lawmakers approved legislation in Maryland to forbid the use of replacement players in Camden Yards.

There were other places that had similar legislations being passed all for different reasons. For example, the Ontario Labor Board concluded on March 28 that the Blue Jays could not use replacement umpires at their home games, so they decided to make their new "temporary" home in Dunedin, Florida. That was their normal spring training site, so if the season was to begin with these new players, the loyal Canadian fans would have had to travel south to see their favorite team.

Was that normal?

To the average player, it seemed normal because they didn't know what was going on behind the scenes, and things seemed to be changing on a daily basis. Just like the rest of the pre-Internet world back then, most of the big stories were broken in the daily newspapers. Some even in the "Late" or "Final" editions, if you are old enough to remember them.

"I would say I played thirty games before they cancelled the season," Riesgo said proudly.

It was Spring Training, and we all know that in the record books the games don't count. Then throw in the fact that many of the players were "replacements," so the games took on an even greater insignificance, unless you played in them, of course.

"There were a number of reasons, there wasn't one specific reason why I crossed. The first being the fact that I was such a strong advocate of the union, including the minor leagues into the union," he said in circles. "Not every player that played professional ball was represented, and that deeply, deeply, troubled me.

"I was adamant in that with my discussions with Donald Fehr (Executive Director of the Major League Baseball Players Association) and mainly Mark Belanger (ex-Orioles shortstop who was Fehr's assistant at the time) on the discussions of including the minor league players."

Clearly this was a heated debate, considering minor league players aren't included in the union today. It steamed Riesgo that "bonus baby players" got paid as members of the 40-man roster even in the minors, but not every player was afforded that luxury. Quite frankly, that was a team's right as an employer, and since Riesgo wasn't one of those players he clearly resented the system.

"I definitely wanted to break their union, not because I didn't believe in the union, I was a strong union man. I think every worker in America should be represented by a union so I am a pro-union. So I wanted to break the union in order to create a better union," he said with the best of intentions. "The reasons were my years of struggles and financial struggles of being a minor league player and not on the 40-man roster for many of those years, and the struggles of raising a family.

"I was out on my own and really homeless for a time right before the '94 strike. I was living in flood control, and kind of sleeping at night beneath some bushes. And I spent some nights lying in the dirt in the back of my parents' house in a little garage area because my parents wouldn't let me in the house. I had a falling out with my parents, and it seemed like the whole world was against me."

So why stick with it? Why cross that line fully knowing that the minute he did, current major league players would brand him forever as a "scab," and unless the game was going to undergo a complete makeover, which it had never done before, he could easily be on the outside looking in.

Here's where the story started. After being drafted by the Padres in 1988, he played that summer for the Spokane Indians in the Northwest League and won a championship there. In 1989, the next season, he played Single A ball for the Charleston Rainbows and completed that. Before the 1990 season, he was traded to the New York Mets, and, shortly after that, he was traded to the Philadelphia Phillies later that summer. After the 1990 season, the Phillies didn't place him on their 40-man roster, so he was selected by the Expos in the

Rule V draft, which is a way for other teams to draft a player who has traveled around the minors, kind of a second-chance program. The catch is the player must remain on the major league roster for a year, or he gets returned to the original team.

Looking back, Damon Nikco Riesgo was a terrific high school player at Long Beach Poly High, and was later the 1990 MVP of the Florida State League representing the St. Lucie, the Class A farm team of the New York Mets. This was the same league that had produced stars such as Johnny Bench, Gary Carter, Cal Ripken Jr., and Mike Piazza, and many others who reached the pinnacle of their sport.

So why did he fail? Why didn't he become a permanent member of some organization?

When the Philadelphia Phillies got him back, they had no room for him, so they sent him down to the Reading Phillies, the team's AA organization, where he hit 14 home runs but his average dipped to .258 in 98 games. The Phillies then released him in the spring of 1992 and the Kansas City Royals picked him up as a free-agent. That put the outfielder's career in jeopardy, and made him an official journeyman in baseball circles. After just one month they sold his contract for a profit to the Mexican League, and Riesgo had to report to Saltillo, Mexico, if he wanted to continue his career.

"They sold me down the river for a profit," he explained. "The Royals had no plans for me and I was totally an opportunity for them to make a quick buck.

"If an organization could get a player as trade bait to possibly enhance their pitching staff, they would do that, and, instead of getting a pitcher, they got cash."

Former Boston Red Sox pitching star Dennis "Oil Can" Boyd had thoughts of crossing the picket line as well. He was a 10-year veteran and stopped playing major league baseball in 1991. With that said, he had nothing to lose, and, at the time, the money that was being offered was obviously attractive to him.

He was 35 years old and was to report to the Chicago White Sox training camp.

Gorman Thomas, a former MLB slugger, was 44, and he was going to give it another go with the Milwaukee Brewers, the team where he became famous for becoming the AL home run leader in 1979 with 45 and was tied with Reggie Jackson of the California Angels for the MLB lead in 1982 with 39.

Thomas did report, but, since he wasn't an active major leaguer, he had nothing to lose, although he had things to gain. He was after some cash and filling personal voids by recapturing the adoration of the fans. Thomas and Riesgo went to that dance via different mindsets, but the money and love of the game connected the two in this comeback venture.

When it was all done, none of these players got back to the big leagues. Boyd and Riesgo continued to play ball in various "professional" leagues, while Thomas hung up his cleats for the final time. This leaves us with the valid question: was it worth it?

Chapter 2

The Business of Baseball

"If you look at minor league baseball and the dollars that minor league baseball teams generate, it's almost the argument of NCAA teams versus the money they generate for football and basketball for the university. Yet minor leaguers, they've created a product, or help to create a product, that they can enhance as players."

Back in the spring of 1995, there was a thought that Major League Baseball had too much influence over the careers of minor league ballplayers. Let's face it, minor leaguers were making paltry salaries compared to their major league brethren, so why not fight for more money? The average shelf-life of a minor league player is short, in most cases, less than six years. After that, they have to figure out what they want to do with the rest of their lives.

Bobby Holley was a California high school baseball superstar, an All-American shortstop at UCLA, and a young player who was looking for some direction and guidance. He first met Nikco at the age of seven and the two planned out a lot of their baseball future together. Even though Riesgo's mind was made up, Holley still wasn't sure what he would do next.

"Only the 1 or 2%, 5% of guys, whatever it is, that can make it six years of minor league baseball, can make any money," said Holley who is currently the general manager and partner of Hardball Warehouse, along with former major league pitcher Greg McMichael. Therefore he has been involved in the business of baseball his whole life in some way, shape or form.

Holley was certainly a forward thinker, and one day he thought to call on Marvin Miller for some advice. Before his stint as (MLBPA) executive director from 1966-1982, Miller was a labor economist by trade. He gained fame by becoming the leading economist and negotiator for the United Steelworkers Union.

"Basically if you don't make it by the sixth year of minor league baseball, you are pretty well shot," Holley added. "If you look at minor league baseball and the dollars that minor league baseball teams generate, it's almost the argument of NCAA teams versus the money they generate for football and basketball for the University. Yet minor leaguers, they've created a product, or help to create a product, that they can enhance as players."

It all sounded good in theory, but Holley had to put his ideas into action and that's when he phoned Miller to ask for a rare meeting. It is safe to say, thousands of former clients phoned the economy icon on a regular basis, and there is no way he could ever meet with them all. There just wasn't enough time in the day, so there was no guarantee that he would even call back, let alone grant a meeting.

"I had a pretty well-honed perspective after having read a couple books. One was *Barbarians at the Gate,* a novel about corporate America, specifically the fall of RJR Nabisco. "I had a lot of information going in, plus coming off the experience of minor leaguers crossing the picket line, that sort of thing."

Holley also had a conversation with McMichael, who was a quality reliever with the Atlanta Braves at that time and a friend and future brother in-law. Their relationship remains strong today, and, even though he never reached the majors, Holley continues to chide his friend about the brief matchups they did have, saying, "I was 3-for-6 against him in my career."

Regarding the conversation they had about the baseball labor situation, Holley recalled, "Yeah we talked. He was holding the party line. I don't think I talked to him about the minor league union at that time. In 1995, shortly thereafter, I got married on October 14, so we weren't fully in the family. I was engaged at the time, so our relationship wasn't like it is today."

Needing something definitive to give him some perspective on whether or not to pursue his union idea past being just a passing fancy, Holley made a phone call that hit the mark.

"I called him up and said, 'Hey Marvin, Bobby Holley. Just some joker guy that played minor league baseball with the Expos would love to meet you. Can I come and visit you? I'm coming to New York.'"

And he responded with, "Sure, come on up."

It was the ballplayer's first visit to the Big Apple.

"I met his wife. She was in and out. I don't really remember a lot of the conversation. He was just kind of re-living what he went through back in the day, and the process of establishing the union," Holley said. "He didn't say either way. He understood the value of having unions. A minor league union wouldn't have the dollars at-play that were at the major league level, so could a group of individuals put something together to make money and develop the kind of clout that somebody's gonna listen to at Major League Baseball?

"It's a hard thing to consider if you look back and see how hard it was to create a major league union. How hard would it be to develop a minor league union unless you have the support of the major league union itself?"

Finishing one last poignant thought about Miller, Holley said, "I think he was a guy that lived a legacy and wanted to help people. That's the perspective I got. I don't think he was going to be out on the party line tooting the horn of a minor league union, but he was going to be willing to give advice, suggestions, that sort of thing."

After the meeting, reality set back in. It was going to take a Herculean effort to get a union off the ground, and real life would start to get in the way of Holley's dream. "I think I was pretty realistic about it. You try to make money for a living and minor league unions aren't going to make money right out of the gate. I got realistic in knowing it was going to be a long process. I wasn't putting too many eggs in one basket.

"After that it was kind of a blur. I don't know if I did a whole lot. I guess in '95 I ended going to Aberdeen, South Dakota, to play in an independent league to keep things rolling. That was in the summer. Then I got married in October, and you know, once you get married, everything's shot. That was my dilemma. I just got married and met with Marvin Miller about this minor league union thing. It was pretty cool, but how are they going to make money? Where's my support?"

Even though Holley became a successful businessman, he still holds a strong affinity for his idea more than a decade gone by. "Oh, certainly. I think it would be great for players to have that support. I'd be glad to run that union to if I had a chance."

Businesspeople with businesses that had relationships with Major League Baseball back in 1995 were starting to get worried about their investments, and what kind of an impact replacement players would have in regards to the future for everyone, which included consumers and fans as well as the business sector.

Pete Cataldo, a writer for www.sportsology.net and hardcore baseball fan, represented most fans that became apathetic towards the sport. He also expanded his scope, coming to the realization that dollars were at risk.

"The owners were ready to start the '95 season with replacement players to "break" the union as owners do in other industries like the air traffic controller strike of 1981," he said remembering that president Ronald Reagan ended the (PATCO) strike where 13,000 of 17,000 workers walked out and had 48 hours to return to work or get fired, and many did get fired, according to an article on www.buyandhold.com by Brian Trumbore. "But in reality, the owners had no intention of breaking the players union. If they had, they would have to lower ticket prices. And all other elements of the baseball experience would become less of a money maker to them, like TV!"

Even odds makers in Las Vegas were worried about the prospect of baseball using replacement players. Living in Sin City at the time, Cataldo had an up-close and personal perspective on this situation.

"Actually, the books let the future bets for the 1994 World Series stand until the series was cancelled. Then they returned them. However, it would have been interesting to see a replacement Yankees team, with perhaps a group of bums, play an Expos bunch, who may have had a pretty good team as well, and the Expos were 50-1 to win the series.

"Depending how the replacements aligned, it could have been a disaster for a fan that had a bunch of money on the Yankees, with a bet he made months earlier. Or a bonanza for some Expos fans that had pie in the sky hopes a year earlier," Cataldo remembered.

"As far as lines for the '95 season, they were posted in some books. In fact, I remember some lines, just a few, and the Yanks and Expos, who were leading the pack in '94, were also favored in '95, despite the books not knowing who their players would be."

Vegas would have to account for the possible return of the regular players and dealing with bettors wanting to place wagers made prior to the start of the 1995 season. "I remember the future bets for the World Series had a stipulation that 90 games had to be played to have action. So the books were ready for action and so was I," Cataldo said confidently.

"I would have loved to have been taken back to my childhood by replacement players in 1995. Once again to see a player who had to earn a living by producing on the field, no set contract, no deferred contract, and he may have had to get a job in the off-season, what a treat that would have been.

"This is the player I grew up with. He signed autographs, lived in my neighborhood, and hustled on every play. But no, the moguls gave in and signed an agreement with the other moguls, and the dollars lived happily ever after. If the owners really wanted to destroy the union, they could have. In fact, by now the level of major league baseball probably would have been back to top shelf."

Going back to the moment at hand, players like Nikco Riesgo realized the pay to be a replacement player would be minimal, but it gave him (and others giving this "opportunity" serious consideration) the chance that he was waiting for, because there was no guarantee that he would ever get another shot at the big leagues.

"They offered what I believe was $100 a day, per game," Riesgo began, "As well as a $5,000 signing bonus if I had remained on the team for opening day. And I would be paid the major league minimum during the season. The major league minimum salary in 1950 was $6,000, which, of course, meant that if you were not in the top one percent of players, you had to have a job in the off-season to live."

He laughed knowing that modern-day players don't have to live like that aforementioned scenario anymore. "In 1994, the minimum was a lot more ($109,000) than the average American earned."

He added, "So instead they formed another union, one of 'let's get all we can' from an owners' point of view, and where the players were also now free to demand salaries that would rival CEO's around the world." From that point on, the salaries started to escalate once again.

Meanwhile, Riesgo did sign his baseball card deal with the Topps Company in 1991, and his Bowman card rolled off the presses as well. That's something every kid dreams of, and, even if he never made it back to the big leagues again, the kid from Long Beach, California, had that to hold on to.

"It would be interesting to know what I did sign," the former ballplayer said candidly. "I was so excited that I never even paid attention to the details of the agreement." Topps had a lot of these contracts and at different times in the 21st century, they sold them to the public because every major leaguer signed them and they were considered collectibles. Riesgo's didn't show up on eBay, most likely because he wasn't a big name, so there's no telling where that document ended up.

"I was like a kid in a candy store." No pun intended from Riesgo with Topps owning candy companies as well. "This was my big league card. I still wear it today, many times around my neck to Little League fields and sporting events. It really gives me a lot of credibility when I sign autographs for the kids, since they have no clue who I am."

The Star company made a 1990 prospect card of the future major leaguer while he was with the St. Lucie Mets. The team had just moved their spring training facility there in 1988, so Riesgo had a chance to play in front of a fan base that was still growing.

"Star cards started off as pretty mediocre quality but as they started to add marquis they got extraordinarily popular for a smaller card manufacturer," said Doug Cataldo, owner of www.cardcornerclub.net.

Most players in that time period got to pocket a cool $75 a year for three years, as part of the company's agreement with Major League Baseball and their Players Association. That deal wasn't making the players rich, but it gave them a presence in the minds of card collectors around the world, myself included, and also gave the kids some valuable information about their favorite players and in some cases their heroes.

Many ballplayers collected various items when they were younger and, in most cases, it gave them a greater appreciation for the game after they made it to the bigs.

"I was fortunate to be a bat boy for the Brooklyn Dodgers in spring training in 1956," former Los Angeles Dodgers All-Star, Steve Garvey reminisced. "Living in Tampa, Florida, my father drove a bus for greyhound and he chartered a pickup for the 'Boys of Summer' at Tampa International Airport to take them to St. Pete to play the Yankees in an exhibition and on that day, in the middle of March in 1956, I fell in love with baseball."

When he started to play the rest fell into place.

"Then I started playing Little League that year and I started collecting cards. I wanted to learn more about my heroes."

Other players idolized a player first and then started to collect every card with them on it. That would start a collection as a result. And most people on this earth have some sort of collection and many of them are baseball card collections.

Baseball is a complex business and the league's success on and off the field directly affects so many other businesses all around the world.

Chapter 3

Looking Back to 1994 and the Cancellation of the World Series

"The team went on an amazing run after the All-Star Game, but then the strike killed the season. It literally killed the team. Fans in Montreal walked away in disgust and never returned. Each day of the strike seemed to peel a layer of love for baseball away from the fans in Montreal."

The 1994 season was an interesting one. The Montreal Expos had a .649 winning percentage, the best in the game. When the season stopped because of the player's strike, they had already played 114 games of the 162-game season.

The season was 70% completed, and if it had ended there, the two best teams were the Expos and the New York Yankees, who had a .619 winning percentage. This was a banner year for the Montreal franchise. They had some terrific veterans, but the key to their success was their scouting department. It was the best in baseball, and they had some of the best young players in the game.

The Montreal roster, which would soon be obliterated due to a lack of strength in ownership and poor attendance when baseball started back up in 1995, was an All-Star team. It was a testament to their minor league system, which was arguably the best in baseball at the time. Only the Los Angeles Dodgers rivaled their Latin country scouting team.

The roster had six Latin players, and that was a lot in those days. Of the six, Moises Alou and Wil Cordero were everyday players, and Freddie Benavides was a utility player. Pedro Martinez, just 22, and into his third season at the time, was the second best starter on the staff. Only Ken Hill, who won 16 games in the role as the team's ace in the shortened season, was better, and Gil Heredia and Mel Rojas were a big part of the team's bullpen. John Wetteland was the team's closer, and he had 25 saves in 52 appearances. He finished an astonishing 43 of the team's 52 games.

Their hitting stars were Alou, the left-fielder who had a .339 average and 22 homers, center-fielder Marquis Grissom who had 36 steals and a .288 batting average with 96 runs scored, and Larry Walker, who had a strong arm in right field, with 19 homers and 86 RBI with a .322 average. Adding Cordero's 15 homers, plus an emerging outfielder named Cliff Floyd, made this team an offensive juggernaut.

It was clearly the best team ever assembled by the Expos, and the last great team to play in Montreal's Olympic Stadium, a venue that was decaying more and more every year. The city dumped plenty of money into the stadium, but they never were able to modernize it the way that it should have been. Toronto built the SkyDome back in 1989, and that had a successful attraction, a retractable roof. It was the first of its kind, and the Expos were looking for the same kind of success that the Blue Jays' home was reaping.

"I've been a baseball fan since I was eight years old, and even though I've never been a diehard fan of the Expos or Blue Jays, (I've always been an Orioles fan), I've always understood how profound it was for the sport in this country when either team did well in the standings," said Canadian magazine writer Baron Bedesky.

"When the Jays won two straight World Series in 1992 and 1993, it directly led to a baseball renaissance in Canada. People who had remained casual baseball fans suddenly became hardcore. They knew all the players. They watched the games on television, at home, and in the bars. They bought Blue Jays merchandise. They talked about the games. Hell, some even had the nerve to argue about baseball as opposed to the usual hockey discussions.

"As a fan of the game, I was witnessing it taking root in the fabric of our pop culture. I know there are some people out there who don't believe in that stuff, but I do. The SkyDome, truly a monument to architecture and an absolute abomination when it comes to baseball facilities, became the place to see and be seen. And I remember thinking at the time, what a fabulous springboard to establishing a second great game in this country.

"Canadian-based minor-league franchises were springing up all over the place. An entire generation of new baseball fans, especially the kids, was beginning to understand the pace and the rhythm of the game, something in stark contrast to hockey, yet never more necessary. Hockey fans were learning how to be sports fans, simply by virtue of buying into the sport that was so fundamentally different from what they had been accustomed to."

The Expos had its diehard fans as well, and their take was always a bit more extreme than the average Canadian baseball fan.

"As an Expos fan, there wasn't as much optimism heading into the 1994 season as there had been in the early 1980's. Baseball was at an all-time high in popularity in Canada, and the Toronto Blue Jays were setting attendance records and were coming off a second straight World Series. Fans even speculated that Toronto and Montreal might even meet in the 1994 World Series," said Jeff Morris, a native of Prescott, Ontario.

"The early 80's Expos had that great pitching rotation with Steve Rogers, Bill Gullickson, Scott Sanderson, and then guys like Charlie Lea or Ray Burris. They had two of the game's biggest superstars in Andre Dawson and Gary Carter. They had incredible team speed with Tim Raines and Rodney Scott. Add guys like Tim Wallach, Al Oliver, Warren Cromartie, and Ellis Valentine, and this team was much deeper than any other Expo team."

"In 1994, a lot of fans were actually negative heading into the season. The team was criticized for trading Delino DeShields, who was a fan favorite, to the Dodgers for Pedro Martinez, who was still considered a prospect at the time. The excitement centered around the outfield. Fans loved Larry Walker, and the fact that he was Canadian made him very popular. Moises Alou and Marquis Grissom were popular, too. Fans in Montreal have always loved speed and a hit-and-run style of play," he added.

As the season went on, many Canadian fans were hoping that the strike could be avoided because their team was emerging as the favorite to win the World Series.

"It wasn't until later in the season that the team really caught fire with the fans. Alou was the big hero in the All-Star Game, and the fans really started to embrace some of the everyday players like Wil Cordero, Sean Berry and Darrin Fletcher. One of the turning points with the fans was when Denis Boucher emerged as a star," explained Morris. "Martinez had won over the fans, and Ken Hill and Jeff Fassero were both solid starters. John Wetteland also gave them the kind of stopper that the early 80's teams didn't have.

"But Boucher, being French-Canadian, started selling out Olympic Stadium every time he started, and he brought the connection between the team and the fans to a whole new level. The team went on an amazing run after the All-Star Game, but then the strike killed the season. It literally killed the team. Fans in Montreal walked away in disgust and never returned. Each day of the strike seemed to peel a layer of love for baseball away from the fans in Montreal.

"The star players all left via free agency or through fire sale. When baseball finally returned, the Expos went from being one of the most promising teams in baseball, to a franchise on a death watch."

The Expos were becoming a big story in Canada, and Major League Baseball literally pulled the carpet out from under those passionate fans, whether they knew it or not. Many of them have never been the same since.

Morris, one of those Canadian baseball fans still taken aback by the demise of baseball in Montreal, added, "I also believe the Expos franchise was highly motivated and inspired by what had taken place in Toronto. The two cities have long had a rivalry on so many other fronts, not only in sports, but economically, politically, and culturally. Citizens in Montreal take great pride in everything they do, and they loathe being outdone by Toronto.

"The Expos management was highly respected, and so they should have been. By 1994, they felt they had assembled a legitimate contender, and a team that would succeed for years. And by August of 1994, they were proving it. From July 18 until the season hit the skids, they went 20-3. 20-3, damn it! When it mattered the most these guys were humming on all cylinders. Then the plug was pulled, just when everyone was working their baseball psyches into feverish pitches once again.

"Well, talk about disheartening! It was like showing your kids all the presents under the Christmas tree, and then handing them to someone else. It was devastating, and the enthusiasm over baseball in Canada has not been the same ever since. Hell, it was the beginning of the end of the Expos franchise. And the attitude toward the game in Toronto has never been the same either. I defy anybody to find one any individual, team, or interest group that was hurt more by that strike than Canada. There's nobody or nothing I can think of."

Pete Cataldo, remembered his first World Series and the implausibility of ever seeing a World Series cancelled for any reason:

"The first World Series I remember is 1950. I vaguely remember sitting in the centerfield bleachers at Yankee Stadium seeing a number "5" moving back and forth in front of me. I was six years old. For the record, that number "5" was "The Yankee Clipper," the great Joe DiMaggio. I remember several years later finding the ticket from that game, and the face value was eighty cents. That's right, less than a dollar to see the Yankee dynasty play the Whiz Kids from Philly."

In his neighborhood the World Series was a cultural phenomenon.

"Growing up in New York in the 50's and 60's, the World Series was an annual event all New Yorkers looked forward to. The Dodgers, Giants, and of course, the Yankees were always in the running for the Fall Classic. So on September 14, 1994, you can imagine my dismay when Major League Baseball called off the World Series due to a strike that had started on August 12 with the Players Association.

"World War I, World War II, the Great Depression and the San Francisco earthquake of 1989 could not prevent America from having the championship of its national pastime decided."

"Here are some of the details of that season that changed the game," Cataldo added. "The Montreal Expos were also killed in the massacre. They were leading the National League with a 74-40 record and may have been the third Canadian team in a row to make it to the Series, as the Toronto Blue Jays won the series in '92 and '93. Keep in mind, a World Series appearance tends to pump up a city for several years with ticket and all other sales, not to mention the attraction of free agents. But just ten years later in 2004, the Expos were no more."

The thought of that still hurts some Canadian baseball fans to this day. One of them is a professional goaltender in the NHL. Martin Biron loves the game and the Expos were his favorite team. He played for the Sabres in Buffalo, a city that is very close in proximity to Canada, and then he played for the Philadelphia Flyers, in a historic baseball city, and is now with the New York Islanders.

"I saw when the plans were made for Montreal (Expos) to start playing some games in Puerto Rico. It was the first day 'til the end. You knew that it was coming that they were getting out of there, and that was bad. Even though they tried to make it look like a good thing, it was a countdown to leave."

The subject brought back a lot of childhood memories of Biron's time at the "Big O" watching his Expos play, but the exodus of the team has made his once cherished memories, bittersweet. The cancellation of the 1994 World Series is still a sore-point for the 30-something netminder.

"Yes, by all accounts that was the year that killed the team. That killed their chance of putting winning teams together," began the goaltender. "You could tell it was coming to that from the years prior to that. I remember I was a 10 or 11 or 12 years old in the late 80's, we used to take bus trips, and our baseball teams used to take bus trips to go up and see the Expos."

One issue that may have led to the demise of the Expos franchise was the team's decision to cap the roof and turn it into a dome. It was cost beneficial to build a roof on Olympic Stadium, avoiding any chance of postponements due to bad weather, but the new addition blocked out the elements as well as the affection Montreal fans had for the ballpark.

"I remember going to Montreal, sitting in the stadium, having the roof open, and sitting at the tower right at the top. It was just a fun thing," Biron said making his point that people go to see baseball games to enjoy the outdoor experience. "It was a combination of things that made the team leave. That, joined with the Canadian dollar dropping, and the fact that they tried to put a roof on that was retractable and the thing wasn't really working right. Now you were basically going to see a baseball game indoors when the season is so short for summer, compared to some of the other markets in Major League Baseball. You want to enjoy the baseball game outside, not go back to a hockey game inside like in the summer. That's not what people were looking for."

After that melancholy memory, the netminder then focused on the good times.

"I remember going to those games and hearing, 'Batting first, the second baseman, De-l-i-i-i-i-no De-Shields-s-s-s-s-s', that got everybody going nuts,'" he remembered. "Marquis Grissom, DeShields, Larry Walker, Andres Galarraga was there for a little bit. Pedro Martinez. John Wetteland. Ken Hill. It was just amazing. I still remember going there at the time of Tim Burke and Gary Carter. I was a big Expos fan. I still have an Expos jersey at home."

This elite athlete still loves the game itself, but now he is a man without a team to cheer for. As you can see, his "favorite" team has been taken away from him forever, but his love for the game keeps his interest in the sport, but not necessarily where Major League Baseball is concerned.

"I am a baseball fan because I love playing baseball. I go see my niece play softball in the summer. I go to minor league ballgames in Buffalo. I've been to Phillies games. Especially since now my son is three and a half, and he is at the age where he wants to play baseball. He wants to hit the ball, he wants to catch the ball, throw the ball or whatever," Biron said speaking as a proud father.

"I was always a big baseball fan that will never leave. I remember sitting down and watching a full nine innings of the Expos. I remember Roger Brulotte. Roger was awesome. I still see him in Montreal going to hockey games and stuff, and I still remember his calls. Like the 'Going, going, gone' (translated to 'Bonsoir elle est partie,' or 'Good night, she is gone') in French was Roger Brulotte. It was his call. It was very, very heartbreaking when they left."

After a short pause, he continued, "Their last summer I remember I went to see a game with my mom and dad in Montreal and there was like 25,000 people. It was very loud that day for that stadium, and I'm like, people are not going to realize it, but they are going to miss having baseball. I don't know if they do or they don't. I mean, I would go to a couple of games a year. You know, once or twice. But for me, when I fly into Montreal and see Olympic Stadium, I think Expos. A lot of people think Olympics, but I think Montreal Expos and those years."

Greed cancelled this great game and the rest of this season for the Expos and the rest of the league. The statistics counted, but it's pretty futile considering there was no end result. Fans to this day remember this non-World Series almost as much as the ones that made so many great highlight reels and DVD's.

Fans throughout North America and around the world were left with an empty feeling. Many of the players were too, but they had the power to do something about it, and at some point it became inevitable that the season was over, and the sport was at a crossroads. Salaries were escalating and attendance was dropping in some markets that used to be strong.

One thing was certain, whenever this strike came to an end the game would need an overhaul, financially and ascetically. Many fans said they would never go to another game again, but only a handful would keep that boycott going as we have learned through the power of hindsight. The game was reeling at the time, but it was poised for a viable comeback.

At this point with the strike in full motion, baseball fans could only read about its progress in the papers, and wait to hear when their sport would be "Open for Business" once again.

Chapter 4

When The Business Runs the Game

"It's pretty amazing what he (Mantle) accomplished and here and now I am in the same shrine as he is in Cooperstown. It's just very, very special."

Baseball is a multi-billion dollar industry that is woven into the fabric of America, and those kids and adults who live and die by the game. Todd McFarlane was a former minor league ballplayer who became well known as the popular comic, "Spawn." He then created McFarlane Toys, one of the bigger Major League Baseball licensees, makers of fine collectible figures. This boss knows his baseball, and his love of the sport made for a great backdrop in the story of his initial foray into producing his collectible products.

"First off, my first contract was with current players. Then it went to retired players, and then it was a little bit of a struggle to get the players in-between, like retired non-Hall-of-Famers," McFarlane said. "I gave them (buyers) three examples: Don Mattingly, Bo Jackson and Kirk Gibson."

Every baseball fan grew up being a fan of the game, but as most get older, they see where the fun stops and the business side takes over, sometimes making the improbable possible.

In the 1984 offseason, Hall of Fame catcher Gary Carter left the Montreal Expos by way of a trade to the New York Mets. After spending eleven seasons in Canada, the perennial All-Star catcher had a chance to shine in the sport's biggest market. By 1985, he was making well over two million dollars a season, so playing in New York had its benefits. As it turns out, New York was the original home of a player that he idolized growing up.

"When I was a kid growing up, '"The Mick"' (Mickey Mantle) was my guy. I always dreamed of what it would be like to play at the major league level," said Carter, who in 2003 was voted into the National Baseball Hall of Fame as a member of the Montreal Expos. "Again I wore the #7 (it was the number Mantle wore in his career), and I never thought when I got to the big leagues, that it would be like it was. I loved the game, had a passion for the game. I have things for my kids. I tried to save them my jersey and last catcher's gear. I have a set of each from the teams that I played for."

Most players like Riesgo strived to be in the same position that Carter described, but most players never get to climb that mountain. Both players played for same organizations at different times, with Carter achieving the better success, including a World Series title with the Mets in 1986.

"It's pretty amazing what he (Mantle) accomplished and here and now I am in the same shrine as he is, in Cooperstown. It's just very, very special," said a modest Carter during his induction into the Baseball Hall of Fame.

Baseball records are something that helps define the sport. Some players don't care what their statistics are until their agent is presenting their case to a general manager while negotiating a contract. That's when something like hitting a lot of home runs can be a golden ticket to some ballplayers.

The legendary gambler and all-time hits leader of Major League Baseball, Pete Rose, continues to be on the media circuit because he holds one of the sport's most sacred records and understands how that achievement affects the business of baseball and sports collecting.

"Baseball records unlike any other sport are sacred, there's no question about it. That's why baseball cards are so much more valuable than football cards, basketball cards, or hockey cards," Rose stated in a recent radio interview on host Howard Eskin's show on famous Philadelphia station, 610 WIP. "It's because of the rich history of the game of baseball, and I just wonder what Ty Cobb or Cy Young or Babe Ruth, who is up in heaven looking down at the game of baseball thinks about the bad stuff in the game right now.

"I know Bud Selig is going to get all of the recognition for cleaning it up, yet everything that has happened that's bad in the last ten years in baseball, happened on his watch. But he's going to get all of the credit for cleaning it up, and I said it last year, I would hate to have his job because what's he gonna do? I guarantee you he wishes Barry Bonds never broke Hank Aaron's record. I can guarantee you that."

"Yeah, but he did nothing with Sosa, with McGwire, and with Bonds to make sure that those sacred records weren't broken," Eskin shot back.

"That's because they were selling tickets," snapped Rose. "After the '94 strike baseball needed something. That's why all the new ballparks that they built are all bandboxes, because they wanted home runs. You know, in 1977, George Foster hit 52 home runs for the Reds, and in 1998 both guys hit over 60, Sammy Sosa and Mark McGwire. So that was the first time in 20 years that someone in the National League hit over 50 home runs, and all of the sudden you have two guys hit over 60? When does the red light go off when these little shortstops are hitting opposite field home runs?"

In 1993, McGwire hit nine homers and did the same in 1994. Both were injury-plagued seasons. Then in 1995, he hit 39 home runs, which was his highest total since he hit 42 in 1992.

In 1994, he earned three million dollars, and that salary was more doubled the following season to $6,925,000. In 1998, he hit a record 70 homers, and his salary rose to over nine million for the next two years after that. In 2001, McGwire's final season, his yearly salary was $11 million.

Players began to see that hitting home runs was the way to cash in big in the sport. No matter how they did it, players who were not sluggers started to re-create themselves as power hitters, and those with some power were suddenly extraordinary. The fans enjoyed this power surge initially, but are now suffering the exorbitant prices to attend and enjoy a baseball game, as well as the stories of performing-enhancing substances that continue to overwhelm the tales of the game to this day.

When attendance goes up, ticket prices go up because of the demand, followed by teams and owners signing very lucrative advertising and television deals. All of these reasons, motivated by the all-mighty dollar, helped bring the sport back from near-death after the strike.

Coming out of a lockout is a tough thing to do. Many wondered whether or not baseball would survive, and it did. When it happened to the National Hockey League, many predicted it would be hurt irreparably.

Kevin Greenstein, editor of www.insidehockey.com said about the NHL's lockout situation, "When evaluating the NHL's remarkable recovery following the 2004-05 lockout, one needs to look no further than the mid-to-late 1990's, when Major League Baseball struggled badly to recover from the work stoppage that canceled the 1994 World Series, and delayed the start of the 1995 season.

Indeed, it took some record-shattering performances, Cal Ripken, the steroid-infused home run derby, to get fans back to the gate. Meanwhile, NHL attendance has risen consistently, and revenues in concert with that, in the three seasons following a lockout that led to wholesale changes to both the on-ice product, and the economic structure of the league. NHL fans may not be as large in number as those for the other three major professional sports in the United States, but their unfailing loyalty is second to none."

The Minnesota Twins almost moved, but cooler heads prevailed and the promise of a new stadium will be fulfilled in the near future. The Florida Marlins were also fighting the same fight to get a new stadium, with a similar threat to move the team to a new city. While the latter team has not gotten their city behind funding a new home for their baseball team, the Marlins continue to stay in South Florida with the hope of getting a new baseball stadium before being forced to relocate elsewhere.

"It's becoming global now, and so many people are passionate about the game of baseball. This is where, I think, the fan gets taken advantage of," said 15-year major league player David Segui. "It's like anything you love. If you are truly passionate about it, you will find a way to make that fit into your budget. The average passing fan? Yeah, that's going to be some of the fat they are going to trim out of their budget when things get tight. There are such a high number of truly passionate baseball fans, that the market is always going to be there, and unfortunately they get gauged and taken advantage of."

Even though the fans pay for the tickets, it's the owners who pull the strings, and eventually get to decide if your city is "worthy" of having a franchise. Baseball isn't the only sport that has had this problem. The NBA had its fair share of teams moving, but none had the outrage that the move of the Seattle Super Sonics had.

The team had the promise of a decent near-future after drafting a star player in Kevin Durant in 2007, and with that, the fans did show up. With that, and the fact the Sonics played in a nice arena, KeyArena, why would they want to move? The team's majority owner Clayton Bennett had decided that he wanted to move a franchise that had done very well in Seattle for 41 years, so it could be in his hometown of Oklahoma City, where his business ventures were based.

Segui played in Seattle for the Mariners and developed a special connection with the Super Sonics. "Now that part of it I don't like. I don't believe in it. I played in Seattle. I used to go to

Sonics games all the time. I purchased tickets. I didn't get free tickets. I bought tickets to go to games. Do the fans have a right to be pissed? Absolutely, because they supported them.

"Now if a team isn't being supported because there is a lack of interest in that sport, that team in that city, then the owner has every right to take his product somewhere else. Now, if they aren't supporting that because you as an owner are putting a garbage product out on the field, or on the court, that's your responsibility just like any other product. You go to the store, and you buy this product. Hey, this is a good price, and I buy it. It's terrible. Do you go back and buy it again? I wouldn't."

It seems very basic, and the fact that this former Gold Glove first baseman still thinks like a fan after pocketing over $41 million dollars in his career says a lot. He understands the common fan and the supply-side economics.

"So now, if you are putting out a good product and people aren't buying it, aren't accepting it, then I think you have the right to go somewhere else. If you put a bad product out there then you are insulting the fan's intelligence, especially if you keep hiking up prices too every year. Then you are insulting their intelligence," he said with true disgust. "What they are saying is, 'I think you are too stupid to notice that I am trying to feed you a terrible product, and I am banking on your passion. I am going to take advantage of your passion for this sport, and I am going to keep gouging you based off of you loving this sport, and willingness to continue to come back.'"

While this isn't prevalent in the sport of baseball, there is a danger that more owners could start to adopt these tactics if they feel they need to "cash in" on the fans with a new stadium, or if they feel the sport may fall on hard times in the future.

When the New York Giants move into their new digs for the 2009 season, the fans paid a "personal seat license" for the stadium.

What does that mean? It gives the licensor the right to purchase season tickets, and if they don't, the team pulls the license. Fans can't buy a partial season license, so the team guarantees themselves all that full-season ticket money in advance, and that's supposed to offset the cost of building a new stadium. Some of their fans paid a staggering $20,000 a seat for the best seats in the house. The Yankees decided against this practice.

But for how long? The Yankees are forking over $1.3 billion in expenses, and with a stalled economy ticket sales may not be that brisk and it could take a long time to pay off the stadium.

The new Yankee Stadium has premium and non-premium seats. The team said that 88% of the non-premium seats sell for less than $100 a seat. When the season started, seats near home plate sold for $500-$2,625 depending how many rows back the seats are. Luxury suites sold for somewhere between $650,000 and $800,000. They fetch the highest prices in the sport for the most expensive ballpark, so it shouldn't take long for this team to be swimming in a sea of green. But if ticket sales slow the PSL talk could start back up just for the premium seating.

Baseball is beautiful, and it's hard to imagine that owners could price the fans out of the sport. However, with the gas crisis and recession of 2008, attendance was down in some cities. So, even a sport as powerful as baseball has to be careful they don't price out the hardcore fans.

Chapter 5

The Call Up to the Expos

"My experience in Montreal wasn't all bad. I got a chance to play against some of the greatest players in the world."

For several reasons, 1991 would be etched in Riesgo's mind forever. Getting top billing was being pulled aside by his manager at Class A ball, Felipe Alou, who told him that he was being called up to play for the Expos.

"My first experience was big. It was on the road in St. Louis, old Busch Stadium, against Ozzie Smith, one of the players I had looked up to all my life. I had met him a few years before in Clarinda, Iowa. He was a former player there, and he would come back for dinners/fundraisers," Riesgo reminisced about his first big league experience. "I was looking forward to playing against him in my first game. It was the bigs and here I am playing against Smith, who is one of the best players in the world.

Ozzie Smith was arguably the best defensive shortstop of his era, winning 13 consecutive Gold Gloves from 1980-1992, a feat that has not been equaled since. Given the nickname "The Wizard of Oz" because of his fielding prowess playing for the San Diego Padres and St. Louis Cardinals, Smith developed his offensive game later in his career, earning a spot in the Baseball Hall of Fame in 2002.

"In my first at-bat, I hit a line shot which I knew was an easy base hit. Lo and behold, Ozzie comes out of nowhere and backhands it with a giant leap. He jumped in the air, spun around, and turned and threw it all the way to first base. I'm not the slowest guy in the world, and it beat me by a hair. That was my welcome to the big leagues."

"I knew just then and there the major difference between the minors and the majors. These plays win Gold Gloves, and eventually win ball games. And you have to be a great hitter to hit .300 in this league. It was everything I dreamed about. There were 30,000 fans. It was just a beautiful day, and everything kids dream about was right there in St. Louis."

That was the good sip of his cup of coffee, but the unforeseen bad sip was yet to come.

"I was a little disheartened when I got to Olympic Stadium for my first game in Montreal, and the 6,000 fans. The stadium still seats around 60,000 fans. It looked like a needle in a haystack. It was really empty which was understandable because the team was 15 games under .500. The team ERA was close to 7.00, and we were just about losing every single day."

Bad seasons seem to bring the worst out of some players, and Nikco Riesgo was no exception.

"So I'm thinking that with my intensity and my style of play, it's something that can rub off and definitely help the team. Obviously that's why they brought me up to the big leagues to play for Expos manager Buck Rodgers and the entire Montreal organization. As it turns out, it may have gone against me," he said in retrospect. "Shortly thereafter, a lot of the players started teasing me because I wore my helmet while I was on the bench with my batting gloves and everything, ready in case they needed me to pinch hit in the first inning for the pitcher, or in case somebody got hurt. My mentality was that I was going to be ready no matter what. I was seeing myself coming in the game, bringing me into pinch hit, driving in a run, helping the team win."

There have been many oddball rituals that players have exhibited in baseball history, but a large majority of them were done behind closed doors. This was clearly unique to baseball and some players didn't take that very well.

"I was there all day long for when they needed me. Then I'd be ready to get a hit or a walk. I was ready to play at all times. From the time the umpire says 'Play ball,' to the very last pitch of the game. That was my intensity every single pitch of every single game. A lot of players saw that this wasn't the baseball way," he said in disbelief even to this day. "A lot of players wear their helmets in football. Me coming up being a football player, my coaches would tell me 'don't you ever take your helmet off.' You might be on the sidelines, but if you have your helmet on, you will always be ready. It's the same thing in hockey.

"Well, I carried that into baseball. It was different, but it always worked for me. If I happened to be starting, if I was hitting fifth or sixth in the inning, I'd be ready. It would let my teammates know 'hey, we aren't going 1-2-3 this inning. It was kind of motivation for my teammates to say we are going to have a big inning. It always started rallies and any team I had ever been on to date, we always won a championship. Sure enough, there I was coming up as the ninth guy in the inning. A lot of guys on the team would rally behind that intensity.'"

While the rookie's superstitious rationale for helping his team was sound and went over like gangbusters in the minors, players in the majors embraced and accepted rituals from veterans. In baseball, as in life, those new to the game have to build equity to get respect from those who have earned that right by paying their dues.

"When I got to the bigs with the veterans and stuff, I was the big joke. They called me 'Helmet.' They would laugh at me. I can handle that it's part of being a rookie. One day I came into the locker room and for some reason, one of the players smashed my helmet to pieces. Somebody threw it back into my locker. He took my helmet, that I had worked so hard in my life to get with so much passion, dedication, and drive, and violated that," he said, still feeling the sting of disrespect and humiliation. "And I wanted to just strangle him, and just knock the heck out of him and beat him blue, and get him the heck off this team.

"It was the big leagues, and there was reason why a team is 15 games under .500 and in last place. When you get guys that are not into the game and winning, it's just a normal day. It's the big leagues, and just getting a paycheck. They are looking at different things they can make a big deal out of that have nothing to do with baseball."

This Expos team had problems besides just having a terrible season. When a rookie is added into the mix of a team going bad, sometimes that addition can produce a spark, mainly because players realize their own expendability, and that change is just a phone call away. However, this team got the wrong kind of spark, and where there was smoke, there was lots of fire.

"So I find out, and it turns out to be Tom Foley, one of the old veterans (exactly nine years counting that season) on the team. Sure enough I am out to strangle him. I wrestle him down and while I am about to punch him, the players are stopping me from absolutely creaming this guy.

"A couple of days later when the news gets to Expos General Manager Dave Dombrowski, I was on my way out with a plane ticket back on my way to AAA," he said with some sadness. "They told me it made me look like I was somebody who wasn't able to fit in with the team. It was controversial, and I was somebody who definitely has aggression."

To this day, Riesgo feels like he never had a chance to tell his side of the story to the organization. It might not have changed their decision, but it may have helped to prevent the scarring that had taken place over the years.

"It was something that nobody wanted to talk about. I would have loved for somebody to come to me and talk about it," he stated. "Their decision was 'there is no talking,' so I have no idea what was their reason was. The reason they told me was, 'Hey, we need pitching up here,' which they did since we were getting killed every day. And how can you argue when somebody says you need pitching?"

The young slugger had lived out his dream by making it to the majors, then had it taken away from him in a New York minute. Besides being left in a bitter state because of the experience, Nikco Riesgo looks back at the experience as something short of a dream.

"My experience in Montreal wasn't all bad. I got a chance to play against some of the greatest players in the world. When the San Francisco Giants came into town, they had Barry Bonds, Matt Williams, Kevin Mitchell, and Will Clark. When the Los Angeles Dodgers came into town, it was Gary Carter, Darryl Strawberry, and Eric Davis. It was just a great experience, and I always wanted to play with the Dodgers," he said espousing the baseball wish of most kids from Southern California. "In my career in the minors, I hit .400 against them."

Riesgo had a chance meeting on the diamond that stuck with him until this day, and helped shape his post-baseball career.

"Carter came over to me to say hi and to give me some encouragement. During the pregame warm-ups he made an effort to say, 'How's it going kid?' and to play hard, and give everything I got and good things will come to me. I'll never forget that day. It made me feel very special and it inspired me to help kids to this day."

Besides getting a chance with the Expos, the random act of kindness from Gary Carter made the whole experience worth it.

Even though Riesgo would never make it back to the major leagues, he will always remember his time there, and he can feel good about his seven-career at-bats and one hit. His on base percentage was .400, so it showed that he had a good eye and he had a knack for getting on base.

Just because his MLB career was brief, it didn't mean that he wasn't able to play the game. Many times, players need that break, some good playing time, and the support of his teammates and his organization. If that doesn't happen, it makes it very hard for a young, relatively unknown player to stick around. Baseball is an exclusive business, and less than a thousand of these baseball specialists exist in the world today.

Any player who gets to play on the major league level was, at one time, the best player in his town, high school, college, junior college, American legion or minor league baseball. Then when they make the jump to the majors, they have to compete with the best of the best. If they don't show much beyond what was seen when they were scouted, that usually equates to a short pro career.

There is no shame in hitting one's plateau and not being able to move up to and stick at pro baseball's top level. This author, and almost every baseball fan on earth, wishes that they had the chance to experience Major League Baseball at some point in their life. Riesgo did experience that, and it was his dream, which nobody can ever take away from him.

Simply put, Nikco Riesgo summed it up in one sentence.

"It was the greatest experience of my life."

Olympic Stadium
Montreal, Canada

Chapter 6

The Final Days of the Montreal Expos

"That year, I don't know how much it hurt baseball overall, but it really killed the Expos. If they had continued that season in '94, I think they would have won it all because they were the best team in baseball that year."

Even though baseball was thriving in 2002, they still had franchises that had to move for whatever reason. The Expos were sold to Jeffrey Loria, a rich art dealer, and once it became apparent that he wasn't going to get a new downtown stadium built in Montreal, he spearheaded a group that bought the Florida Marlins. As a consequence, the league's owners then became the proud new owners of the downtrodden Expos, a once proud franchise.

"It was a good place to play. There weren't huge crowds, but when we played good baseball it seemed like they would come out," said former Expos second baseman Delino DeShields. "Still just a special place to come up as a player.

"That year, I don't know how much it hurt baseball overall, but it really killed the Expos. If they had continued that season in '94, I think they would have won it all because they were the best team in baseball that year."

Loria and his group took the team's computers, which had their scouting reports, out the door. Major League Baseball never lifted a finger to make a move to stop them, which was a shame since the Expos had the best scouts and many of the league's best prospects at that time and over the years.

The franchise lasted just two more seasons, playing part of their home schedule in San Juan, Puerto Rico, and the rest in Montreal. Back then entering Olympic Stadium felt like visiting a relative's house after a loved one had just passed away. The Expos didn't know it, but they were already dead. The obituary just wasn't written for them yet.

The "Big O" was a marvel back in the 70's, but, even then, it was a stadium in disrepair. It was like that 1970's car you are holding on to because it's paid off, but the bumper is dented and the vinyl interior is cracking. When I bought a program for the game, the one-page foldout was hot off the Kinko's presses, and you could feel the workmanship that was put into it.

The 1969-2002 Yearbook was packed with Expos history and touched on the current players. The fact that it was the 1969-2002 Yearbook was a bad sign because not many teams celebrate a 33-year anniversary.

When you got past the happy security staff that spent their quality time checking their bank balances daily to see if the checks had cleared. You came to the ticket rippers, who were the original guys, and they were nice despite waiting for the inevitable.

The Expos had the recently acquired All-Star pitcher Bartolo Colon on the mound that day against the New York Mets, and the attendance read 13,000 strong. That's right. It took just a few minutes to clear the place since the two upper levels were "closed for the season."

As right-fielder Vladimir Guerrero hit yet another game-winning homer, and the Expos were on the winning side of the ledger, the piped-in crowd noise really gave fans chills. NOT! It was yet another misguided decision by management to create artificial excitement, and it came off as cheesy as a doo-wop group opening for Van Halen.

As the playoff-constructed Expos sat on the fringe of the playoff hunt, Major League Baseball had already given up the team's future in a bunch of "now" trades. MLB said at the time that the Expos had a $40 million dollar budget and were operating at a loss of $30 million. The bookkeeping didn't make sense considering the team was owned by the other 29 teams in the league.

The levee finally broke and the Expos packed up and moved to Washington D.C. Fans from the outside looking in believe Expos fans didn't care, and that's why only 5,416 showed up to their next to last game in Montreal. The main fact was, the fans had been seeing this coming for years and couldn't emotionally invest themselves in a franchise that was stripping away its talent for years, knowing that their leaving was inevitable.

I interviewed various Expos players over the past few seasons, and they wanted this. They wanted to move. They wanted a franchise that would spend money, and they didn't want to have to travel to San Juan anymore. That was a nightmare for the players, but the owners did that to make as much money as they could that season before the franchise was sold. The team had a budget and once they decided not to spend $50,000 to call up players in September when they had a chance at a Wild Card berth in 2003, the fans and the city lost. Washington, D.C. eventually got the franchise.

The Expos played their last game at Olympic Stadium on September 29, 2004, losing 9-1 to the Florida Marlins and former owner Jeffrey Loria. They drew 31,395 fans, a far cry from the 43,739 the stadium was capable of holding for baseball games. The club's last game in the history of the franchise was an 8-1 loss at Shea Stadium on October 3, 2004.

Shea's usefulness would be exhausted after the 2008 season, in favor of a new stadium known as Citi Field, also to be housed in the borough of Queens, as its predecessor was.

On April 8, 1969, 35 years prior to their final game, the Expos played their first-ever game in New York as well. The franchise had come full circle, and ended their run with 2,755 wins against 2,943 losses, and four ties.

Baseball is a great game and an equally complicated business. Fans never thought about the business back in the 50's, but are very aware of it now. The Expos fans were the big losers, and they never followed another team. Their heart was with the Expos and when the franchise left, they gave up on baseball.

Expos fans will forever remember Bill Lee, Gary Carter, Tim Raines, Warren Cromartie, Rusty Staub, Randy Johnson, Pedro Martinez, Andre Dawson, Vladimir Guerrero, and a whole host of other superstars that passed through the franchise and Olympic Stadium, now a "billion dollar dump," which is only used by the Montreal Alouettes of the Canadian Football League for playoff games only. The 2008 Grey Cup, the CFL championship game, may be the last great event at that stadium.

Chapter 7

Former Teammates Whose Paths Would Never Cross Again

"Bop was the best second baseman I have ever seen. He played with great speed and power that was very uncommon for a second baseman."

Nikco Riesgo played with some great players while he was in Montreal, and one of the more talented players was a young man from Seaford, Delaware, named Delino DeShields. In 1987, the Expos selected the young speedster with the 12th overall pick in the amateur draft.

"Bop was the ultimate teammate," Riesgo recalled. "I read about him in *Baseball America* as one of the Expos' top prospects and was excited to play with him."

"The lower rounds, rookie ball, A-ball, they are still kind if focusing on the draft picks and giving them a chance to play. But once you reach AA, dude, you gotta play. I don't care who you are. Eighth round, 10th round, 20th round, the best players are going to advance," DeShields stated.

DeShields was 18 at the time. Just out of high school, the team wanted to get him signed to a deal and into their system. Even though the game was changing back in the late 80's, one thing that was still prevalent was the fact that many players that were drafted didn't have an agent or anybody who could represent them, so decisions were made on the fly.

"I got my contract in the mail. I didn't have an agent. I got it in the mail, and I sent it back in the mail," he said candidly, fully knowing that today, that would never happen. "The day after I graduated from high school, I was on a plane headed to Bradenton, Florida.

"So there wasn't a whole lot of negotiating, and seeing what this guy's got and all of this. This is what they offered and I said 'ok'. Four years of college and they threw that in. That was it. It was like, 'lets go and play ball.'"

As of 2008, there were only 48 major league players born in Delaware in the history of the game. DeShields is clearly the best positional player of that bunch.

The other notables from that part of the country was a pitcher who later turned into a top-flight manager for the 1980 World Championship Philadelphia Phillies, Dallas Green. Green was better known for the latter than his playing career by a wide margin.

Another pitcher, Chris Short, was a player for the Phillies back in the 50's. He managed to win 20 games once and he was a two-time All-Star.

One of the other notables were Hans Lorbert, an infielder of the last century (who once raced a quarter horse around the diamond and lost); Dave May, an outfielder who played in the 70's; Kevin Mench, a millennium slugger, and, Randy Bush, a part time player for the Twins. They were all good players, but DeShields had a chance to be a real difference maker at the light hitting position of second base.

"I found out real fast that I wasn't as good as I thought I was," he laughed. "There was another variable, and that was the Latin variable. And also the Asian kids that we don't get to see. Those guys can play, man, and there are a lot of them.

"I saw some stuff that I hadn't seen on the ball field before. It was definitely a little bit of shock, but not intimidation."

In 1990, DeShields' rookie season, he had 42 steals and a .289 average with the Expos at the age of 21. He had a terrific chance of winning the Rookie of the Year Award, but a young Atlanta Braves outfielder named David Justice had come out of that team's farm system. Justice won the award providing his team 28 homers and 78 RBI. Despite the near miss, the young second baseman would improve.

DeShields and Riesgo crossed paths early that season, and DeShields took a liking to the new 24-year-old prospect. This is when the veteran of just one season was hoping his younger teammate would stick around for a while.

"When I got the call to play in the Big Leagues, DeShields was one of the first players to welcome me to the team and reached out to make me feel comfortable. It is always nerve wracking meeting new teammates, because you never knew how they will receive you."

"We hit it off right away," DeShields remembered. "Nikco was a good guy, and for me, I can't speak for everybody, I am always pulling for the guy that is not the consensus All-American or top dog, so to speak. The underdog."

Before DeShields came into the game, Cincinnati Reds great Joe Morgan (lifetime 689 steals, 1,133 RBI, 286 home runs) or St. Louis Cardinals great Rogers Hornsby (lifetime 1584 RBI, 301 home runs, .358 lifetime average) were the two second basemen who were unusually great players for that position. Otherwise, most second baseman had to field well, run well, bunt and hit second or eighth in the lineup most of the time. DeShields had the ability to drive the ball, or steal a base to get himself into scoring position. His career lasted just 13 seasons, but he did have an impact on the sport.

"Bop was the best second baseman I have ever seen," Riesgo added. "He played with great speed and power that was very uncommon for a second baseman."

In 1993, the Dodgers had their eye on the speedy DeShields, and, sure enough, they traded a skinny pitcher named Pedro Martinez in order to get him. His tenure as a member of Los Angeles was interrupted by the strike.

"You know I got traded for Pedro that winter, and I was in L.A. Really, that Expos team, it was just a matter of time.

"As young players you are never for a strike, I don't care what the veterans are saying, and how it will benefit later. You can't even see that far a lot of times as young players."

He was a player that thought about the game before himself, but, as time went on, he realized there were some benefits of the strike.

"It didn't hurt my career," he said after recalling the impact that the strike had on the sport. "Looking back at it now, I guess it did some good. Salaries increased, but, as far as the Montreal Expos, that was the worst thing that could have ever happened.

DeShields finished, "Because we were young players coming up. You know, '94, '95, that was going to be *our* time over there."

DeShields had so much potential, and it was evident when the Dodgers traded one of the best prospects they have ever pushed through their system. Pedro Martinez would become one of the greatest pitchers in his era.

Oddly enough, there was very short list of African-American Dodgers who played second base after the legendary Jackie Robinson, which made DeShields proud to know that he was playing for the same franchise that broke the color barrier. Like most black kids, Robinson was a mythological figure he looked up to and later had a chance to emulate on many levels.

"I am a history dude, and he started in Montreal, then went to L.A. and actually played for the Dodgers. This is all stuff that I will take to the grave with me. They are experiences that you can't buy anywhere. It was definitely something that I thought about."

By 1995, it wasn't clear if DeShields would have a long career, and, in retrospect, he was productive for five more seasons. After that he kicked around with the Cardinals and Cubs for two more years until he hung up his spikes at the age of 33.

DeShields isn't bitter, but he has thought about what his career would have been like if there wasn't a steroid scandal.

"I don't want to sound like a hater, but not just myself, but there are many guys that have been victimized by the drugs in the game," he said honestly. "Guys that you outplayed annually ever since you first came in to rookie ball. Then all of a sudden, this guy pops up and hits 40 home runs. It's not right. It didn't just affect me, it affected a lot of guys.

"My thing is, that I can't believe that baseball, overall, wasn't aware that this was going on. I'm not gonna believe that."

Riesgo's path was a lot bumpier, and by 1995, it was on life support. He was still a very good player and had promise, but he was running out of time. He was 28 years old still trying to live out his dream, but the clock was ticking. He needed to get a stable career going at some point. He had a family to support, and semi-pro baseball didn't exactly pay top dollar.

Just like any other cat with nine lives, Riesgo had a few of them left. Yet, he never thought he wouldn't get another shot at the bigs. He was too positive, and he just never thought that way.

Chapter 8

What's Next?

"I tried all the way through May of 1995. I kept at it every year I kept at it. I would say for literally five years. I kept myself in shape."

Nineteen ninety-five would prove to be an interesting and frustrating year for Riesgo. He was still playing baseball, and, four years removed from the majors, so he decided to play ball for an independent league.

"I went down in 1995 to play in an independent league for the Alexandria Aces. They had the Texas-Louisiana League back then. What an interesting time that was," he recalled. "So when I couldn't find a major league job, I figured, 'let me go and play here, I would get some at-bats in and stay in shape.' When I went there I had such a bad experience. They signed me, and then they released me."

Once again the kid from California got another shot in the gut, but like a boxer with tons of heart, he kept coming back.

"After the halfway point, after I led the team to 18 straight wins, and we won the first-half title, they decided they could save money since they were already in the championship, because they had won the first half of the season," he said talking about his release from the Aces. "I was the highest paid player. I was so upset about how they treated me that I stayed in town for nearly three weeks, and I waited for all of the other teams to come into town so I could talk to them."

Basically he marketed himself to the locals, which was a smart move. All of a sudden he went from being a player to a fan again, and the people who cheered for him now sat next to him.

"Alexandria was a great place to play, a great little ballpark. A great little fan base. They would get 5 to 6,000 fans a game."

Hanging around did get the attention of former Major League Baseball star Jose Cruz. Cruz had a solid 19-year major league career, mostly with the Houston Astros. He was a two-time All-Star and now he was a manager looking for a slugger.

"Jose Cruz was one of my guys who really heard me and listened to me. He was coaching the Laredo, Texas, team at the time, so he came into town to play the Aces. Through my experience in the game, I knew if I was in town, at the ballpark, somebody was going to sign me because I hit the ball 400 feet," Riesgo said proudly.

"It was a bit of a distraction for the home fans because I would be there signing autographs, and the kids would come up to me. He said, 'hey, we are in last place and I need you, so will you sign with us?' I said, 'absolutely I am ready to play, so let's go.' I said it's a new second half, and we could win the second half."

With a never-say-die attitude, he took on his new challenge with a new team, and had a chance to stick it to his old team. Who wouldn't relish a chance to do that?

"So I was leading that team in first place and hitting .400, and I hadn't seen a pitched ball in like a month, really. I was hitting everything I see in the first two weeks. Just kind of furious and mad about how I was treated and looking forward to winning the second half for Laredo. We were in last place, and now we were in first in the second half," Riesgo stated.

"Laredo was hurting. When I was there, it was just a small rinky-dink ballpark. Not like the Alexandria ballpark. They were getting hundreds a game and maybe 1,000 if it was a good night. The worst night was probably 100 fans. It was pretty sad."

Once again it seemed like the writing was on the wall for Riesgo, who was 28 years old at that point. Baseball is a tough business, and the further you get away from Major League Baseball the harder it is for those teams to turn a profit.

"What happened was they were in such bad financial condition because of the first half, the owner decided to pull the plug in the second half and not give Cruz a chance. The whole team went bankrupt. They stopped paying the players. They stopped paying the coaches. I literally played two weeks like 10 games for them," recounted Riesgo on his rough journey in the independent leagues. "So all of the sudden the team is out of the league, every player is going home, and I was like, 'Listen, I'm not going home. I'm sticking around again. I will go find another team and finish out this season.' I think the owners made the decision to pull the plug even before I was signed. They just couldn't make their minds up."

So now he was on two teams. Was there going to be a third? Could the league stay afloat?

"So the league decided to have a draft because of the players being out of jobs. Basically the players could be drafted by the other teams in the league. So I was thinking maybe I would get drafted by one of the teams. As it turns out another team out of Lubbock, Texas, drafted me. They were the Lubbock Crickets," he said.

The interesting footnote about that team was it was named after its most famous resident, the late, great singer Buddy Holly who fronted The Crickets back in Rock 'n' Roll's heydays. Their home games were played on Dan Law Field on the campus of Texas Tech University.

"It was interesting that they had won the first half of the other league, so they didn't really need me, but they wanted me just because I knew everything about Alexandria, about some of their weaknesses. They were looking for any advantage they could in order to beat them," he said regarding his familiarity with his former team, "which is kind of a smart move on their end. They really didn't play me, they had their team already, they really didn't need me, and their loyalties were to the players that they had that won them the first half. They got me just to beat Alexandria."

Now that he was on a new team, he wasn't playing for the money. His main directive was being there to take care of some unfinished business.

"My pay was $1,800 a month, and afterwards I took a cut to about $1,000 a month," he remembered. "They wanted me as insurance, and to know about their pitchers, etc. I was a scout and just a thorn in their side."

Players want to play and when that doesn't happen, sometimes success isn't that sweet. Being a team player is all well and good, but, in the real world, most players are only willing to take a hit in playing time to win it all just once in their career. The reason being, they never know when that career might suddenly be cut short.

"Actually I got some at-bats," he said with some glee in his voice. "They would put me in some crucial situations. Once in a while I got a start. That was frustrating because I wanted to play every day, but I understood. I was a team player and I understood."

He was a good soldier and was still getting paid. Well, sort of, but he had a chance to win a championship, and that's hard to do at any level. Most players never get a chance to have that experience just one time in their career.

"I hit a couple of key home runs and key doubles in the championship series, and we won the whole Texas-Louisiana League championship."

Here is the kicker: he left town after finishing his business, and never looked back.

"I left town without my ring. I just donated it to the team," he said with sadness in his voice.

He had just won the championship against the team that unceremoniously released him, and should have been dancing a jig at the feat, but, instead, he felt unfulfilled. The struggle to get there possibly played into his lack of happiness over a seemingly great achievement.

In the end, he didn't get to reach his potential, and, if he were used more, he might have felt like he was a bigger part of the success. He was more of a chess piece the team played to mate their opponent.

After that championship, the team just faded away like so many others in that league. The league followed and became the Central Baseball League. The new incarnation lasted until 2005 when they disbanded for the final time, and as a consequence, some of those teams went on to form the United League which is still operating today.

"I tried all the way through May of 1995. I kept at it every year I kept at it. I would say for literally five years. I kept myself in shape."

Riesgo was once again looking for a baseball job and now his options were beginning to dwindle. What was he going to do next?

Chapter 9

Nikco's Connection with the Fans

"I loved signing autographs. I think I signed over a million autographs it was just who I was."

For as long as there have been baseball players, there have been fans trying to get player autographs. It's a natural phenomenon that surrounds every athlete in every sport. In America, baseball players will always hold a special place in the hearts of their fans, and most players know that. The players tuned into this fact do whatever they can because of the realization that the fans are the ones that pay their salaries.

Some players give a little piece of themselves with each signature.

"I loved signing autographs. I think I signed over a million autographs. It was just who I was. I wasn't one of those guys that passed a kid and said I didn't have time for them and said 'I gotta go'," Riesgo said with great sincerity. "I was one of those guys who would come out and look for kids when I knew I had a few minutes for them before a team stretch or something like that. There are always a few minutes in the day where I knew I had some time to give back to the kids, so I would make myself available."

Some players feel that fans are too intrusive and, because of this fact, don't sign any autographs, or limit the amount of signatures they give away. It doesn't necessarily matter how famous a player is, it's more about their personal choice to sign or not. Or is it?

"I would sign as many as I could. I cherished the celebrity and the limelight, and it gave me motivation. It was my inspiration to really get out and give it my best. I loved it, and it's a part of the game."

Nikco Riesgo got it, but he also knows he wasn't mobbed like some of the players he saw when he was a young player with the New York Mets' organization.

In the summer of 1985, New York's ace pitcher Dwight Gooden's Topps rookie card was a "must have" if you lived in the area.

There was a frenzy that ensued when he broke into the league. He and teammate Darryl Strawberry signed free autographs for many New Yorkers. Some stars signed for free at times, but behind the scenes, some would also look to cash in on that fame.

Given the environment of the capitalistic advantages of celebrity, and the ability to cash in big from the scribble of the name their parents gave them at birth on a piece of paper, baseball, etc., could you really blame them?

"A lot of players use their autographs to make money. I would see Darryl Strawberry coming up with the Mets and he would be signing. He would probably sign a thousand balls, and all of those balls were meant to be sold. He would sign cards and pictures and all of those were going to be sold. It was a business. It was a way to make extra money," Riesgo remembered. "It was the same for Pete Rose and other stars. They would literally sign thousands of balls at one time.

Rose is one of the most sought after autographs on the market, and yet there are plenty of them out there to choose from.

If you pony up the cash, that is.

With his being ousted from the game, this is his livelihood since he cannot currently work in Major League Baseball. Even when he was manager of the Cincinnati Reds, and being paid handsomely to do so, Rose still signed because it was a lucrative side gig, at best.

"They considered their autograph a moneymaker for them, so when it came to the kids asking for a free autograph they were like, 'Hey, wait a second, that's a free autograph, no?' You can get my autograph by going and buying one of those baseballs.

"So it was more of a money thing to some players, and for me, I never got to the point where it was a money thing."

By the time Riesgo came in contact with him he was already an eight-year veteran.

"You know I think if I would have made the million dollar club with the Strawberrys and the Pete Roses, I think I would have stayed the same just because I looked for that celebrity and I loved being in the limelight," he said honestly.

He added, "I probably would have signed a thousand balls just to sell the balls, but then I would have signed another thousand just for the kids because they happened to be at the game that day supporting the team."

It's a clear-cut case of supply and demand. Some players were so beloved that they could never keep up with the supply, and especially the demand. A player in Riesgo's situation was much different. He was a major leaguer, but he wasn't a star and, for the latter, different rules applied.

Some players are angered when they believe a fan is selling their autograph. They have tried to combat that over the years by personalizing their autographs, while others will only sign cards with only their name. Some won't sign bats and balls that same way.

There really is no way to end it all unless the player decides to not sign at all. This reluctance to sign an autograph usually causes negative press, which does more damage than good for the player.

Should players care if fans sell an autograph or two, really?

"I wouldn't care if they sold it. If they can make one hundred bucks or a thousand bucks, life is tough out there, and they have their own lives and have to make a living," Riesgo stated.

Anybody who has ever collected anything thinks in the same way as Riesgo. Some players who were never collectors don't understand why fans want them. In fact, it's a small percentage of people who can generate cash these days from some stray autographs that they might collect. Even if they print a certificate of authenticity by copying it with an excellent home printer, consumers have gotten sophisticated and generally want photographic evidence when they are paying for an autograph.

The other issue is, some players scratch out their autographs when they are free. Some are almost unrecognizable, while other players use their initials only. When a collector pays those same players, the autograph suddenly looks considerably better. It's hard to sell a crappy looking signature, which is another way players have figured out how to control things.

Many retired players are more than happy to sign. Most of them are happy just to be recognized, and in most cases, they give fans a perfect autograph because they might care a little more than the younger player who is a lot more popular.

"I'm in baseball, so I am making plenty of money making a living, and I'm not going to worry about the guy making some extra bucks. That's something where we live in America, and they have the opportunity, and that's what its all about," he said like a true entrepreneur.

If every athlete had this opinion about this subject, most sports would have a bigger fan base. If players dis a few fans along the way, those fans would spread the word. Many of these fans have kids, and if they pass around this information about these players, it can then negatively impact their sport. This doesn't happen immediately, but it can happen over time, and this is not a good thing to say the least.

Chapter 10

Mixed Messages

"It was the championship building Phillies. All the nucleus was there with Lenny Dykstra, John Kruk, Ricky Jordan, Wes Chamberlain, Dave Hollins, they really had a team that was ready to compete for the World Series," he said knowing now that it happened three years later.

When a player interviews with a member of the media, there are a lot of things at play. The journalist is looking for a story, but he is also looking to get it right. If the subject matter upsets the athlete, there is nothing that person can do. That is, unless there is a misunderstanding and that player is misquoted. It happens every day of the week, and it happened to Nikco Riesgo as well.

In the fall of 1990, the New York Mets traded Riesgo and a minor leaguer named Rocky Elli, to the Philadelphia Phillies for an aging second baseman named Tommy Herr.

Herr was born in Lancaster, PA, and was signed by the St. Louis Cardinals in 1974. He was never drafted, but became an All-Star and, in 1985, was a key member of the St. Louis Cardinals World Series team that lost to the mighty Kansas City Royals in seven games. He was very productive that season considering he hit just eight homers. Even with that low output of home runs, Herr drove in 110 runs. He was deadly that year, but had his ups and downs at the plate. In the field he was one-half of a deadly double play combination that included the "Wizard of Oz," Ozzie Smith, and first baseman Keith Hernandez, and later slugger Jack Clark.

In 1989, Herr played 151 games for the Phillies, but his production was down to two homers and just 37 runs batted in. In 1990, he had played in 119 games before the trade, and his production was better: hitting four homers and 50 runs batted in, and 21 doubles. During that time the Phillies were a sub-.500 team, and the Mets were in the midst of a pennant race. The thought was an experienced player like Herr had a chance to help a team down the stretch.

Riesgo was a power hitter for Class A, St. Lucie, and, in 1990, he led his team with 14 homers and 94 runs batted in. He hit .298, and he had 35 doubles and 46 stolen bases. The outfielder/first baseman was quite simply the star of the team, and that's why the Phillies wanted him. The first baseman of the 1990 team was Ricky Jordan, but he was having a power outage with just five homers in 324 at-bats, so they were looking for a power hitting first baseman. Riesgo fit the bill.

"It was really a great weekend for me. One of the Mets fans, who followed my career basically down in St. Lucie, with the St. Lucie Mets, was able to set up transportation and everything to go to Philly and see the last games of the series. "See how they do and just give me a chance to see the team, which was great for me since the organization just traded for me," Riesgo said, now that his minor league season had ended. "They traded Tommy Herr and they wanted me and I wanted to take a look at Philly because I didn't know too much about Philly.

"I was a fan basically. I was just there in the stands. I was there and some reporters were there and knew that I was in town so they were asking me some questions. The Phillies didn't pay for me to come. I just paid for everything myself. I was a Florida State MVP with the Mets, and the season was over for me. I was ready to help a team win the World Series. I was ready to help the Mets."

The Mets needed something else, so Riesgo was hoping he could become a member of the Phillies' 40-man roster. If he could make it onto that roster, he would finally become a major leaguer. Since it was late in the season, he also saw an opportunity to get some at-bats and try to impress his new team.

"That would have been sweet. I was there, so it was a good opportunity for me to be there. They could need me. I had a family too, and I needed to be playing and I was the best player at the time (in the Florida State League) over Pudge Rodriguez, Mike Piazza, Kenny Lofton, and Jeff Kent. I broke many records, and I led the league in, like, eight offensive categories.

"It was the championship building Phillies. All the nucleus was there with Lenny Dykstra, John Kruk, Ricky Jordan, Wes Chamberlain, Dave Hollins, they really had a team that was ready to compete for the World Series," he said knowing now that it happened three years later.

"I would be out there early helping players warm up and stuff. Dave Hollins and I got to be real close. We knew each other from the Padres. We were teammates. He was like my blood and my brother, and we knew if we were playing together that day we would score a couple of runs, him and I together. It was good to have him around."

But his trip to Philadelphia would take a surprise turn for the worse.

"So I was in town and a few reporters came up to me, but one guy puts in the paper (*The Philadelphia Daily News*), he asked me a few questions: about what I thought about, if I could play and things like that, and was I very confident? Absolutely. I was in the best shape of my life and I was ready to play, and ready to help the team get to the next level and get to the World Series. That's the goal for the team."

And the reporter asked, "What about John Kruk and Ricky Jordan? They are great players, too." Riesgo replied, "I am here to help. I talked about my speed. I thought I had good speed. I stole over 40 bases, so of course I am going to say I have good speed and good power. I had good power numbers. So I said my numbers take care of themselves, and even with Ricky Jordan, I am confident that I can help this team win."

Some reporters and most fans think certain players are cocky when all they are is confident. A player must have that swagger to survive in the game of baseball, and, sometimes in the press, that can be misconstrued.

"So it comes out in the paper the next day and the quotes show off a little bit of confidence, but some of the players definitely could have read it as the way it was written. I can't recall exactly how it was written, but it was somewhere along the lines where I felt that I was better than John Kruk and Ricky Jordan, and that I would be the starting first baseman next year and wherever they play, it's up to them. Something like I was better than both of these players."

This didn't sit well with his prospective teammates.

"I think I heard some whispers and controversy from some of the players like John Kruk saying something like, 'Who is this guy? Now this guy thinks he is just going to come in here and start?' I was just, like, wait a second. I didn't say all of this stuff. And it really affects the players and how they are received when it's their first impression with the team.

"So when it came down to it, they decided not to sign me. They didn't even protect me by placing me on the 40-man roster, which was kind of surprising, and meant they weren't going to invite me to spring training."

Why wouldn't a team include a power hitter with speed on their roster? There had to be some other things at play.

"I don't know if that was because of all of the reporters - that would have been intense. I was not welcome on the team. They (the reporter) just started a controversy with teammates going into camp.

"I think if I was the owner, and I was on the team, and I was one of the players, and a guy comes in and all of a sudden I read in the papers that he's starting at first, he's better than everybody, I would be, like, 'Let's hold off this guy right here for a second. And we'll see what happens if he gets picked up.'"

Whatever the team's plan was, he didn't get picked up. In hindsight, would he have done anything differently?

"No I can't say that. There are guys like Barry Bonds who say 'I don't talk to reporters,' and 'I don't do this,' and I'm, like, 'listen you guys, let's go hunting and fishing together. What do you want to talk about?' I don't run away from reporters.

"Hopefully someone would call me in and say, 'What are you thinking? What happened with this guy?'"

But in fact, nobody in the Phillies organization ever gave Riesgo a reason as to why they didn't retain his services.

"No, nobody knows. When it comes down to it, there are a million other players trying to challenge for your position. It's cutthroat. A lot of things are just hearsay and gossip, and you have to rationalize and have some type of understanding.

"With some of the things, you look back and reflect on, and say, 'Hey, maybe if it wasn't worded this way, I could have been protected by the Phillies, and went to camp with the Phillies. And I would have never went to the Expos, and we would have won the World Series in 1991.' You never know what's in the minds of owners, and what they are doing. So I had a lot of unanswered questions. Where was I going to play and where was I going to be?"

Chapter 11

Change Could Help the Game

"It's a scary leap and it's a tremendous amount of work. I think they have just been kind of blinded by the opportunity."

Earlier in the book, the idea of including minor league players to the big league union was a dream for former minor leaguer Nikco Riesgo. The main objective for this plan was that it could secure minor league players financially before making it to the majors.

"I would say value. You immediately place a value on your players," he said speaking about the entire professional baseball populous. "Now, if a major league player makes, let's say for example, a million dollars a year, a minor league player could possibly make a half a million dollars a year. Now that entire minor league marketplace has value as far as the players go, and place value in said marketplace at, at least, half the price of what they pay the major league television market.

"Why isn't every Triple-A game on a network? Why isn't every Double-A game on a network? Why isn't every Single-A game on a network? Why isn't every single pro game on a network that represents organized baseball that can now be marketed across the globe? We are now looking at growth for the union."

This would certainly make the union grow, and instead of having minor league players worrying about their finances, they could focus on their craft and where they are headed. There would be more certainty, and a nice salary would be a constant for them.

Some will say that this will take the hunger out of the players, but others might say this would give the players more independence and free them from the strong controlling grip of the owners.

Owners might fight this idea at first, but if they could pull in more finances from their minor league teams, then it would stand a chance of passing. Finances run the sport and, if all 30 owners agree that this would be good for them, this proposal would certainly be a part of the sport's next collective bargaining agreement.

"We want to take the game global, and teach millions of kids the game of baseball. I think the union can have a great role in that if they include the minor leaguers into the union, and put value in them and increase the revenues. It could grow into a real global baseball league," he said like a true dreamer.

This could all still be a dream that hasn't a prayer of being taken seriously, or it could be implemented immediately. If the players decide they like this, then they form a unified front and push for it and, if they're lucky, get the fans behind the idea as well.

The reality is, a great deal of major leaguers aren't financially secure for the rest of their lives, until they either get a big signing bonus or get a few years of major league service under their belts.

This change wouldn't affect the current arbitration structure, it would merely add another layer to protect the players who give their collective hearts and souls to the game, but never make it past the minors. This plan would also allow minor league ball players to have longer careers, which could increase attendance and baseball fans' connection with players because more players would be able to stay with one organization, not a common practice in the modern era of baseball.

"I'll never forget Mark Belanger's last words to me, and bless his heart. He had a heart attack through the strike because it was so stressful, and he was so adamant on his position, but he clearly asked me 'Why in the world would a Wade Boggs give anything or care anything about someone like me, a minor leaguer?'"

Belanger was a former shortstop for the Baltimore Orioles, and former assistant to Donald Fehr, who runs the Major League Baseball Players Association.

Those words from Belanger were harsh towards a minor league player like Riesgo, but they had a lasting effect on him for the better. It was at that point that he realized that he was a member of the Boston Red Sox on paper alone, and, unless he was called up to the majors, that many of the players on that team would not give him the time of day.

"And that stuck with me. Why would somebody be so adamant that a major league player has no care in the world whatsoever for his teammate, someone in his organization? That told me right there, 'Listen something is wrong here.'

"It was so stressful for him by just not giving a damn! It was an adamant voice of resistance. How can you resist your organization? When you win a World Series you win it as an organization. You don't win it as individuals. Does one person win it? Your whole organization got you that World Series win."

That statement is the cold, cynical reality all ball players deal with until they make it. Some get to experience that euphoria, while many others don't. Most fans probably don't realize the plight of the minor league player and what they have to go through, risking injury to get possible riches down the road when they sign a major league contract. It's not just handed to them, but even if they do everything right, they still might not get paid.

"It's a scary leap and it's a tremendous amount of work. I think they have just been kind of blinded by the opportunity," Riesgo said in a strong way.

"I think the union and the owners just haven't sat together and drawn up the business model, and drawn up the future of the possibilities. Including the minor leaguers into the union, what cost that would represent, and the revenues associated with that is something that needs to be done."

Coverage of minor league baseball is limited to local media outlets. Could that change? There is always the possibility that games start to become readily available, but that would take more advertising dollars and corporate backing to make that happen.

The game of baseball still has the opportunity for more growth. With more growth comes more fans and revenue. Some of that growth could come from building a concerted effort in the minor league markets. Another would be seizing youth interest in the sport away from football and basketball, baseball's biggest adversaries in the battle to encourage younger athletes, from the inner cities and beyond, to join their ranks.

Globally, baseball is taking a hit from a host of other sports. Baseball lost its stronghold as the favorite pastime in the United States. It holds that title just by name at this point. If the minors offered up the luxury of allowing talented foreign players spots on their rosters to allow them the chance for seasoning and participating in the game up close, those players would bring a contingency of fans, young and old, from their native countries, to the game itself.

Some countries, like Cuba, still partake in an oppressive stance when it comes to their athletes, hence, forcing some to risk their lives to defect, by any means necessary, to play major league baseball. These players, the North American professional leagues don't have the jurisdiction to welcome into an open market of welcoming, but those in Japan, Dominican Republic, and others could have the chance of being professionals in the top baseball market in the world.

"It took almost 100 years to get instant replay, so I don't know," Riesgo said, contemplating the great length of time a transition like this may take. "I don't know. I would like to say immediately.

"They made a big effort here on the steroids with the Mitchell Report, and they've wrapped that up in a nutshell. It's over with, and that's because everybody came together immediately."

Nikco Riesgo could be right. However, the only way something like this can happen is if both sides sit down and agree on it. This isn't the first time the owners and players have heard this idea. It was put out there over a decade ago, and still there hasn't been any change.

Major League Baseball has a chance to make a landmark decision here since there is no other sport that has the same structure they do.

The National Hockey League has the American Hockey League, but that's a totally different league, with a different commissioner.

The NBA has their development league, but nobody watches those games.

The NFL uses colleges as their feeder system, so baseball is on its own island.

Major League Baseball started their drug testing in the minor leagues, and, again, that happened expeditiously. If the right people sit down and read this, the hope is that they might feel that this idea has merit, which would be a step in the right direction.

Or any direction moving forward.

Current Revenue Sharing

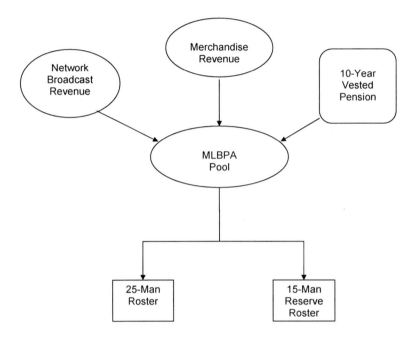

Proposed Revenue Sharing

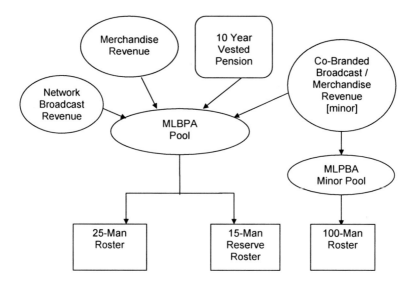

Key

Network Broadcast Revenue: Network and radio revenues earned through broadcast games.

Merchandise: Revenues earned from team logo merchandise sales.

10-Year Vested Pension: Major League Players Pension.

MLBPA Pool: Profit sharing disbursed to players from earned revenues resulting from broadcast games and logo merchandise.

Co-Branded Broadcast/Merchandise Revenue [minor]: Revenues earned from network broadcast for co-branded minor league games and co-branded merchandise sales.

Co-Branded: MLBPA and owners agreement to brand Minor League ball clubs with their logo on uniforms and merchandise.

25-Man Roster: Roster of contracted major league players for any given American League or National League team.

15-Man Reserve Roster: Roster of signed reserve minor league players prepared to step in for any player on the 25 Man Roster.

40-Man Roster: [not displayed] Roster of combined 25 Man and 15-Man Reserve rosters.

100-Man Roster: Roster of minor league players not currently benefiting from revenue sharing.

MLBPA Pool: 40-Man Roster players' share of earned revenues.

MLPBA Minor Pool: Players' share of earned revenues.

Chapter 12

New Beginnings

"The tennis balls really are a lot harder to hit than hardballs because tennis balls are smaller."

Damon Nikco Riesgo has been through a lot over the years, and even though he hung up his spikes in 1995, he has been busy trying to spread the joy of baseball to anybody who will listen.

"Right now I have my global baseball youth academy, which I have setup on twelve acres of land, in the heart of Oakland County, Michigan, one of the wealthiest per capita household counties in the nation," he said with pride. "We have thousands of baseball players here who want to play in the big leagues."

It's all about having that dream and getting the proper instruction so they can get to the next level. Many times players have the talent and the desire but sometimes they need a tweak or two in the mechanics.

Sometimes they just need a break.

A former player like Nikco has connections, and just a positive word from a former player, to another former player who might be a General Manager or scout in the big leagues, can pay big dividends.

"The youth academy gives them an opportunity to play year round," something hard to do in Michigan with Mother Nature's having to dump snow in the area during the winter months. "It's a dome that has world class field turf, and every single day we are hitting and kids will take 1,000 swings a day. They also throw 500 pitches a day as far as target practice.

"When they aren't using baseballs. They are using tennis balls, which are much lighter and allows them to stretch out their arms. The tennis balls really are a lot harder to hit than hardballs because tennis balls are smaller."

Are the tennis balls being used for more than one reason?

"Every once in a while we will throw a bullpen session when a pitcher is ready. It's about training and maintaining insurance. The thing about using a hardball is you don't want to use that with kids as young as we have them. One of them is four years old. The academy's official ages range from seven to 21 and over."

Using tennis balls has been a preferred training method by many Major League Baseball players however; Alex Rodriguez chose to use hardballs in that machine. As a young player with the Seattle Mariners, Riesgo had a chance to work with the future Hall of Famer and it certainly helped his hitting. Even a player with a sweet swing like Rodriguez's understood the importance of practice.

"I have worked with A-Rod and other major league players," he stated as a matter of fact. "I've been training, really, ever since I was a player. I love to talk about hitting with other players.

"I trained A-Rod for about 20 minutes with one of the first spitters, which is an automated soft toss machine. When it first came out, I was hitting with different camps and setup a camp there with A-Rod when he was young and with the Mariners. He would come up there and I would say 'basically this is the greatest machine in the world' and I rattled off about 400 line drives across the field. I was hitting line drives off the wall, over the wall, just about everything.'"

This is something that the team invited Nikco to do.

"Larry Beinfest was the Director of Player Personnel and he asked me how many machines I brought to camp and I told him I brought nine, but sold just one. He said 'I'll take them all' and he wrote me a check for all eight of them on the spot."

Ken Griffey Jr. was on that team as well, but there was a reason that Nikco didn't work with him.

"I worked with A-Rod because he wasn't really the superstar Griffey was at the time," which makes sense and then he continued, "Griffey had a lot of people around him, reporters and things like that. It was hard to get close to him and A-Rod was coming in. I also knew one of his hitting instructors from the Florida State League together, and we would talk hitting and he introduced me to A-Rod."

"He (A-Rod) smashed the ball like crazy. I hit the ball on the field where you could see my line drives all over the place, but A-Rod did his workouts into the net. That's why I love to take the machine out to the field. I tell these guys if you hit on the field you can see if it goes into the corner, or if it twists and where it goes, and read the spin on it. You can't do that just hitting it into the net."

So getting back to his current business, he outlined what he has the youngsters do on a daily basis.

"So everyday we are here, and we are running like crazy. One of our work mottos is 'Nobody works harder than us.' We start the day stretching and we hit the base paths. From home to first, first to second, second to third, and third to home."

But that's not all the taskmaster, who has been known to run on rare occasions, seems to like the sound of the whip cracking.

"We do 50-yard coordination drills. We sprint 50 yards up, and 50 yards back. We race backwards 50 yards...As far as coordination, I want to make sure the kids are working on this as well as fundamentals and their skills."

With this technique, it's understandable how Nikco developed the speed to steal bases. It was based on a lot of hard work.

"After that we all head to home plate," said the leader. "We do what's called a 'suicide' (as if every athlete reading this hasn't done them in some way, shape or form), where we go from home plate to second base, and back to home, and then home to the infield center....until we go from home to center field, we call the "green monster" here and we time it. And these kids run that four to five times a day."

This is a technique that requires dedication, and the willingness to do things that will bring great rewards to those who push the hardest in the end. Something only a former player who worked hard at his craft would understand and create.

"It's just awesome to see them work on the running and endurance, and their speed," he said gleefully. "We have had a couple of kids lose 10-20 pounds that came in here and never knew baseball, and they are starting to look like some baseball players.

"A lot of kids say on their first day that their bat speed is amazingly fast. We do swing. We swing, like, 1,000 swings a day with each player because I teach the kids how to swing and hit the ball without a ball being pitched. It's called a 'shadow swing.' So they will do a couple of hundred and just rattle them off."

Tennis balls can whip in there but are they faster than a baseball? If so, is that part of the challenge?

"It's the size, mainly. Not necessarily the speed," Riesgo chuckled. "You have to have 20-20 vision to hit that tennis ball on the sweet spot. We do some defensive drills, and we have a game called one ball, one bat.

"It can be 4-on-4 or 8-on-8. It's a game situation where kids are pitching to each other, hitting the ball. There are no strikeouts and everybody gets to the plate. The defense is live so you have to run on anything. But if they throw the ball on the infield you have to stop at that base. We try to avoid rundowns and people getting injured. We do rundowns in a separate drill. I jump in there once in a while to show them what to do."

Riesgo knows the good teams in baseball practice and talk about everything, so they are never put in a situation they haven't talked about. But, hey, this is baseball. Things happen in every game the viewers and, sometimes, the players have never seen before.

"These are spring training drills, and that's how you can tell a good team from a bad team, with how they do their rundown. When you get that player in a rundown you want to get that out. It's a key skill in baseball that is sometimes overlooked," he said speaking from his inner manager.

"I think chalkboard time is missing about everything that you can possibly talk about strategically in baseball. It's done on the good teams and on bad teams, when they are in a slump, they can get in the room and strategize.

"For example, a team may have to strategically eliminate the other team's speed to win. One way to do this is to setup multiple throws to the base when a runner gets on. Video is a key component now in the locker room, trying to find weaknesses. That's the environment that I am trying to bring in here. We are all on the same page."

This kid from California has literally spanned the globe in hopes of continuing his career as a player. When that dream ended, his focus took a left turn, but with some hard work and ingenuity, he has managed to stay close to his first love - the "grand ol' game" of baseball. It's in his blood.

References

http://sports.espn.go.com/espn/print?id=1347770&type=columnist
    ("Case of the Missing Computers")
http://www.baseball-almanac.com
http://www.Baseball-reference.com
http://www.ebay.com
http://www.mlbpa.org
http://www.Retrosheet.org
http://www.sabr.org
http://www.toppsvault.com
http://www.Wikipedia.org

Index

Aaron, Hank, 24
Aberdeen, South Dakota, 11
Alexandria Aces, xx, 43-45
Alexandria, Texas, 43-44
All-Star Game (1994), 2, 15, 17, 18
Alou, Felipe, 29
Alou, Moises, xii-xiii, 15, 17
American Hockey League, 58
Anderson, Sparky, 3
Angelos, Peter, xxi, 4
Atlanta Braves, xi, xii
autographs, 13-14, 44, 47-49

Barbarians at the Gate, 10
baseball collecting, 14, 24
Bedesky, Baron, 16
Beinfest, Larry, 64
Belanger, Mark, 5, 56
Benavides, Freddie, 15
Bench, Johnny, 6
Bennett, Clayton, 26
Berry, Sean, 17
Big O. *See* Olympic Stadium
Biron, Martin, 19-20
Boggs, Wade, 56
Bonds, Barry, 24, 32, 54
Boston Red Sox, xxi, 2, 56

Boucher, Denis, 17-18
Bowman baseball cards, 13
Boyd, Dennis "Oil Can", 4, 6-7
Bradenton, Florida, 39
Brooklyn Dodgers, 14, 19
Brulotte, Roger, 21
Buffalo Sabres, 19
Buffalo, New York, 19, 21
Burke, Tim, 20
Burris, Ray, 17
Busch Stadium, 29
Bush, Randy, 40

Camden Yards, 4
Canadian baseball fans, 16-21, 35-37
Carter, Gary, xii, 6, 17, 20, 23-24, 32, 37
Cataldo, Doug, xv
Cataldo, Pete, 11-14, 18-19
Central Baseball League, 46
Chamberlain, Wes, 51-52
Chicago Cubs, 42
Chicago White Sox, 6
Citi Field, 37
Clarinda, Iowa, 29
Clark, Jack, 51
Clark, Tony, 4
Clark, Will, 32

Cobb, Ty, 24
Co-Branded, 59-61
Co-Branded Broadcast, 59-61
Cohen, Russ, xv-xvi
Colon, Bartolo, 36
Colorado Rockies, xii
Cordero, Wil, 15-16
Cromartie, Warren, xii, 17, 37
Cruz, Jose, 43-44
Cuba, 58

Dan Law Field, 45
Davis, Eric, 32
Dawson, Andre, xii, 17, 37
DeShields, Delino, 17, 20, 35, 39-41
Detroit Tigers, xxi, 3
DiMaggio, Joe, 19
Dombrowski, Dave, 31
Dominican Republic, 58
Dunedin, Florida, 4
Durant, Kevin, 26
Dykstra, Lenny, 51-52

El Paso Diablos, xxi
Elli, Rocky, xx, 51
Eskin, Howard, 24

Fassero, Jeff, xii, 17
Fehr, Donald, 5, 56
15-Man Reserve Roster, 59-61
Fletcher, Darrin, 17
Florida Marlins, xiii, 26, 35, 37
Florida State League, xx, 6, 52
Floyd, Cliff, 16
Foley, Tom, 31
40-Man Roster, 5, 52-53, 61
Foster, George, 25

Galarraga, Andres, 20
Garvey, Steve, 14
Gaston, Cito, 4
Gibson, Kirk, 23
Glavine, Tom, 2
Gooden, Dwight, 47
Green, Dallas, 39-40
Greenstein, Kevin, 25
Grey Cup, 37
Griffey, Jr., Ken, 64
Grissom, Marquis, xii, 15-17, 20
Guerrero, Vladimir, 36-37
Gullickson, Bill, 17
Gwynn, Sr., Charles, xviii-xix
Gwynn, Tony, xviii

Hardball Warehouse, 9
Heredia, Gil, 15
Hernandez, Keith, 51
Herr, Tom, xx, 51-52
Higginson, Bobby, 4
Hill, Ken, xii, 15, 17, 20
hockey compared to baseball, 16-17

Holley, Bobby, 9-11
Hollins, Dave, 51-53
Hornsby, Rogers, 40-41

independent leagues, xxi, 11, 43-46

Jackson, Bo, 23
Jackson, Reggie, 6
Japan, 58
Johnson, Randy, 37
Jordan, Ricky, 51-53
Justice, David, 40

Kansas City Royals, xx-xxi, 6, 51
Kent, Jeff, 52
KeyArena, 26
Kruk, John, 51-53

Laredo Apaches, xxi, 44
Lea, Charlie, 17
Lee, Bill, 37
Little League, xv-xvi, 14
Lofton, Kenny, 52
Long Beach Poly High, xviii, 6
Long Beach, California, 13
Lorbert, Hans, 40
Loria, Jeffrey, 35, 37
Los Angeles Dodgers, 14, 15, 17, 32, 41
Lubbock Crickets, xxi, 45

Major League Baseball. *See* MLB
Major League Baseball Players Association. *See* MLBPA
Mantle, Mickey, 23-24
Mantle, Russ, xv
Martinez, Pedro, xii-xiii, 15, 17, 20, 37, 41
Mattingly, Don, 23
May, Dave, 40
McDonald, Michael, xi-xiii
McFarlane, Todd, 23
McGwire, Mark, 24-25
McMichael, Greg, 9-11
Mench, Kevin, 40
merchandise revenue, 59-61
Mexican League, xxi, 6
Miller, Marvin, 9-11
Milwaukee Brewers, xx-xxi, 6
Minnesota Twins, 26
Mitchell Report, 58
Mitchell, Kevin, 32
MLB, xx, 1, 9, 11, 14, 21, 44, 48, 58
MLB Strike (1994), xi, xxi, 1-5, 24-25, 33, 41, 56
    affects the Montreal Expos, xi-xiii, 3, 15, 18-21, 35-37, 41
    cancels 1994 World Series, xi, 2-3, 19, 25
    fan reaction to, xi-xiii, 1, 15-21
    oddsmakers bets during, 12

reasons for, xi, 1-2
MLBPA, xi, 3-5, 9, 11-13, 55-57
MLBPA Pool, 59-61
MLPBA Minor Pool, 60-61
Montreal Alouettes, 37
Montreal Expos, 23
    affect of 1994 strike on, xi-xiii, 3, 15, 18-21, 35-37, 41
    demise of, xxii, 18-19, 35-37
    play games in Puerto Rico, 19, 35
    Riesgo plays for, xvii, xx-xxi, 29-33, 39
Montreal, Quebec, 18, 20, 21, 29, 33, 36, 41
Morgan, Joe, 40-41
Morris, Jeff, 17-18

NBA, 26, 58
NCAA, 9-10
network broadcast revenue, 59-61
New York Giants (baseball), 19
New York Giants (football), 27
New York Islanders, 19
New York Mets, xv, xx, 5-6, 23-24, 36, 47, 51-52
New York Yankees, xii, 2, 12, 14,15, 19, 27-28
NFL, 58
NHL, 19, 25-26, 58
Northwest League, xx, 5

Oakland County, Michigan, 63
Oklahoma City, Oklahoma, 26
Oliver, Al, 17
Olympic Stadium, 16, 18, 20-21, 30, 33, 35, 37
100-Man Roster, 60-61
Ontario Labor Board, 4

PATCO, 12
performance enhancing substances, 24-25, 42, 58
personal seat licenses, 27
Philadelphia Daily News, 53
Philadelphia Phillies, xi-xii, xx, 5-6, 21, 39, 40, 51-54
Philadelphia, Pennsylvania, 53
Philadephia Flyers, 19
Piazza, Mike, 6, 52
pitching machines, 63-64
Puerto Rico, 19, 35

Raines, Tim, xii, 17, 37
Reading Phillies, xx, 6
Reagan, Ronald, 12
replacement players
    Dennis "Oil Can" Boyd, 4, 6-7
    experiences of, 3-5
    forbidden to play at Camden Yards, 4
    Gorman Thomas, 6-7

Nikco Riesgo, xxi, 1, 3-5
    pay of, 13
    replacement umpires, 4
Repoz, Craig, xx
Riesgo, Nikco, xv
    advocates MLB union, 3
    as a replacement player, xxi, 1, 3-5, 13
    awarded: All-American, xix, xx; Florida State League MVP, xx, 6, 52; National High School Scholar Athlete, xix, xx
    base stealing by, xvii-xviii, 52, 65
    creates Major League Players Organization, xxii
    drafted by: Lubbock Crickets, 45; Milwaukee Brewers, xx; Montreal Expos, xx, 5-6; San Diego Padres, xx, 5
    fights Tom Foley, 31
    free agency of, xx-xxi
    intensity of, xviii, 30-31, 63-66
    interest in breaking MLB union, 5
    major league goal of, xviii, 1, 29-33, 42
    managed by: Buck Rodgers, 30; Charles Gwynn, xviii-xix; Felipe Alou, 29
    MLB debut of, xx, 29
    nicknamed "Helmet", 31
    on attendance at Olympic Stadium, 29
    perceived overconfidence of, 52-54
    playing minor vs. major league baseball, 29
    plays baseball, in youth, xvii-xviii
    plays for: Alexandria Aces, xxi, 43; Charleston Rainbows, 5; El Paso Diablos, xxi; Laredo Apaches, xxi, 44; Long Beach Poly High School, xviii, 5; Lubbock Crickets, xxi, 45-46; Montreal Expos, xvii, xx-xxi, 29-33, 39; Reading Phillies, xx, 6; Saltillo Saraperos, xxi, 6; San Diego St. University, xix, xx; Spokane Inidans, xx, 5; St. Lucie Mets, xx, 6, 52
    released by: Alexandria Aces, xxi, 43; Boston Red Sox, xxi; Laredo Apaches, xxi, 44; Philadelphia Phillies, xx, 5-6
    retires from baseball, xxi
    runs youth baseball academy, 63-66
    signed by: Kansas City Royals, xx, 6; Milwaukee Brewers, xx
    signs baseball card deal, 13

Riesgo, Nikco *(continued)*
    sold by Kansas City Royals, xx, 6
    sold to Saltillo Saraperos, xx, 6
    thoughts on: autographing, 47-49;
        Delino DeShields, 39-41;
        developing a minor league
        union, 4-5, 55-57; global
        reach of baseball, 55-58;
        Ozzie Smith, 29; reporters,
        53-54
    traded by: New York Mets, xxi;
        San Diego Padres, xx
    traded to: Boston Red Sox, xxi,
        56; Detroit Tigers, xxi; New
        York Mets, xx, 5;
        Philadelphia Phillies, xx, 5
    wins: Northwest League
        championship, xx, 5; Texas-
        Louisiana League
        championship, xxi, 45-46
    works with Alex Rodriguez on
        hitting, 64
Rightnowar, Ron, xxi
Ripken, Jr., Cal, 6, 25
Robinson, Jackie, 41
Rodgers, Buck, 30
Rodriguez, Alex, 64
Rodriguez, Pudge, 52
Rogers, Steve, 17
Rojas, Mel, xii, 15
Rose, Pete, 24, 48
rosters. *See* 25-Man Roster; 15-Man
    Reserve Roster; 40-Man Roster;
    100-Man Roster
Roy, Jean-Pierre, xii
Rule V Draft, xx, 6
Ruth, Babe, 24

Saltillo Saraperos, xxi, 5
Saltillo, Mexico, 6
San Diego Padres, xx, 6, 53
San Diego St. University, xix, xx
San Francisco Giants, 32
San Juan, Puerto Rico, 35-36
Sanderson, Scott, 17
Scott, Rodney, 17
Seattle Mariners, 26, 64
Seattle Super Sonics, 26
Seattle, Oregon, 26
Segui, David, 26-27
Selig, Bud, 24
Shea Stadium, 37
Short, Chris, 40
SkyDome, 16-17
Smith, Ozzie, 2, 29, 51
Sosa, Sammy, 25
Spawn, 23
Speier, Chris, xii
Spokane Indians, xx, 5
Spring Training (1995), xix, 2-5
St. Louis Cardinals, xx, 29, 40, 42, 51

St. Louis, Missouri, 29
St. Lucie Mets, xx, 6, 14, 52
St. Petersburg, Florida, 14
Star Company, 14
Staub, Rusty, 37
Strawberry, Darryl, 32, 48
strike. *See* MLB Strike (1994)

Tampa, Florida, 14
10-year vested pension, 59-61
tennis balls, practicing with, 63-65
Texas League, xxi
Texas Tech University, 45
Texas-Louisiana League, xxi, 43, 46
Thomas, Gorman, 6-7
Topps Company, xv, 13-14
Toronto, Ontario, 18
Toronto Blue Jays, 4, 15-17, 19
Trumbore, Brian, 12
25-Man Roster, 59-61

unions, 5, 9, 12. *See* MLBPA
    minor league, 4-6, 9-11, 55-58,
    60-61
United League, 46

Valentine, Ellis, 17
Van Horne, Dave, xii

Walker, Larry, xii, 16-17, 20
Wallach, Tim, 17
Warr, Dean, xv
Washington, D.C., xiii, 36-37
WDEL radio, 2
Wetteland, John, xii, 15, 17, 20
Whiz Kids, 19
Williams, Matt, 32
Winokur, Jeff, 2
WIP radio, 24
World Series (1950), 19; (1985), 51;
    (1986), 24; (1991), 54; (1992) 16,
    19; (1993), 16, 19; (1994), xi, xxi,
    2-3, 12, 15-21, 25
www.cardcornerclub.net, 14
www.insidehockey.com, 25
www.mlpo.org, xxii
www.sportsology.net, xv, 11

Yankee Stadium, 2, 19, 26
Young, Cy, 24

Index by Sumner Hunnewell

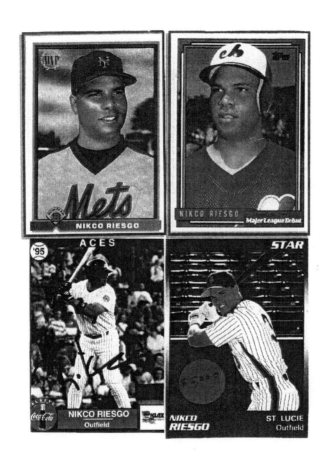

DANIEL F. DUQUETTE
EXECUTIVE VICE PRESIDENT / GENERAL MANAGER

April 1, 1995

FOR PURPOSES OF UNCONDITIONAL RELEASE
OF A TEMPORARY REPLACEMENT PLAYER

American League

Mr. Damon Nikco Riesgo:

You are hereby notified that, pursuant to Paragraphs IV and XIX of your Major League Uniform Temporary Replacement Contract ("Replacement Contract"), the Boston Red Sox Baseball Club is terminating your Replacment Contract and granting you an unconditional release. We shall promptly forward a check that covers all compensation that is owed to you under your Replacment Contract. You are now free to negotiate and contract with any other Major League Club or any other professional baseball team.

The Red Sox understand the trying circumstances under which you played while the Major League Baseball Players Association ("MLBPA") was on strike. We want you to know that we sincerely appreciate the valuable services that you provided to the Red Sox during this difficult time. You were an important part of our effort to provide Major League baseball to our fans in the face of the MLBPA's strike. Your contribution will not be forgotten.

We wish you the best of luck in your future endeavors, whether they are in professional baseball or some other line of work.

Sincerely,

Daniel F. Duquette,
Executive Vice President and
General Manager

Received: X 4-1-95 , 1995

By: X _____
Damon Nicko Riesgo

cc: Dr. Gene Budig, American League President
 Mr. Bill Murray, Major League Baseball, Office of the Commissioner

BOSTON  **RED SOX**
FENWAY PARK 4 YAWKEY WAY BOSTON, MASSACHUSETTS 02215
617-267-9440

June 7, 1995

Damon Riesgo
3552 Gaviota
Long Beach, California 90807

Dear Nikco,

    Enclosed please find your copy of our 1995 team photo from Spring Training.

    I trust that you have fond memories of this historic spring of 1995. You helped to keep our great game of baseball alive during this most difficult time for our National Pastime.

    All of us in the Red Sox Organization thank you for your help and support and wish you the best in your future endeavors.

                        Sincerely yours,

                        Daniel F. Duquette
                        Executive Vice President and General Manager

DDF:mw
enc.

1995 Boston Red Sox Replacement Team

LaVergne, TN USA
27 January 2011
214185LV00001B/43/P